DIVIDEND INVESTING PLAYBOOK

HOW TO BUILD RELIABLE INCOME AND WEALTH - EVEN IN TOUGH MARKETS

RILEY WHITMAN

Published by SYNAST PUBLISHING

ISBN: 978-1-968418-07-6

INTRODUCTION

Dividend investing stands as a beacon of financial stability and growth, offering a pathway to steady income amid the turbulence of fluctuating markets. The essence of dividend investing lies in its ability to generate reliable income and build wealth over the long term, leveraging the power of reinvestment and compounding returns. This book is crafted as a comprehensive guide for anyone seeking to harness the potential of dividend stocks, regardless of their level of experience or the size of their initial investment.

Readers will find a clear and actionable roadmap to constructing, managing, and expanding a dividend portfolio. This guide addresses common apprehensions about the complexity and perceived risks of dividend investing, dispelling myths that it is reserved only for retirees or those with substantial capital. Instead, it offers a structured approach that balances the pursuit of income with the potential for capital appreciation, illustrating how dividend investing can fit seamlessly into various financial goals and life stages.

The book is underpinned by real-world research and feedback from a diverse community of investors, ensuring its content is both relevant and practical. It promises a global perspective, with strategies applicable to investors in the US, UK, Canada, and Australia, enriched with up-to-date examples and devoid of unnecessary jargon or sales pitches. Readers will be equipped with tools for tax optimization, risk management, and automation, as well as strategies for navigating market downturns with confidence.

This is not a narrative of instant wealth but rather a testament to the enduring power of patience, discipline, and informed decision-making. By the end of this guide, readers will be empowered to transform their financial landscape through dividends, achieving peace of mind and financial security, even in challenging economic climates.

Table of Contents

Chapter 01: The Power of Dividends

Historical Significance

For a very long time, dividends have supported and contributed to the profits and stability of investors. Throughout the centuries, building wealth has largely depended on this strategy that rewards shareholders with part of the company's profit as dividends. When focusing on the history of dividend investing, one should keep in mind how it played a part in forming worldwide investment thinking and patterns.

People have been using dividend investing since the first days of the stock market. By giving dividends to shareholders in the 17th century, the Dutch East India Company established a practice seen in corporate management for years to follow. This method was important for sharing the company's success and also helped create trust among those who financed the business.

When markets changed, dividends came to indicate how financially stable and healthy a company was. Back then, both 19th and 20th-century companies decided to pay dividends in order to gain and maintain the trust of investors. Back in the Great Depression, firms that still or increased how much they paid out in dividends were highly admired for their strength in tough times. Back then, investors realized that receiving dividends became a key source of income when gaining capital from stock was difficult.

Dividend Aristocrats show that growing dividend payouts are highly valued by companies that manage to keep up the practice over a long period. These businesses are regarded as strong in the market and provide investors with peace of mind in getting a steady income. Looking at the success of Dividend Aristocrats highlights why dividend investing remains popular; it promotes steady income and progress over time.

Also, dividends have made up a major share of returns from the stock market in history. Lots of research has revealed that over time, the earnings from dividends and their reinvestment have boosted the returns in stock portfolios. Other investors find this rewarding in times of market instability, as the payments are reliable and steady.

Lately, dividend investing has become more popular because of shifts in the economy and the population. Since most developed countries are getting older, more individuals are looking for ways to earn income from their funds. Through dividends, retirees have a way to get income without selling their assets.

To sum up, dividend investing has made an important history because it has evolved consistently with the ever-changing needs of the market. It's still a useful choice for those who want some income and rising value, thanks to the reliable returns that dividends have always provided. Because of this legacy, experienced and new investors follow the same approach to financial safety.

Market Stability

The stability of the market helps shape successful strategies that investors wish to use for the long term. Stability in the market plays a key role, especially for people who look for dividends on their investments. Because dividend-paying stocks keep earning income, you can get a steady income from this type of investment during times when the market is uncertain.

To put it simply, market stability describes how well financial markets can handle unexpected changes and shocks from outside. This type of market is calm, so there aren't sudden and unexpected changes in prices. Those interested in dividends need the market to be stable so dividends continue to be reliable. When the market stays stable, companies usually pay or raise their dividends, making the income for investors dependable.

It is easier to plan your future when you're confident about how the market will behave. Reinvesting dividends becomes easier as investors are sure that the core stocks are unlikely to have drastic changes in price. Since it is reliable, people can make a plan for building wealth and concentrate on their future aims instead of adjusting to daily market shifts.

More importantly, stable markets encourage investors to increase the diversity of their investments. To reduce risk, investors should use diversification, which means investing in several sectors and different countries. When the market is stable, investors are certain that diversifying their holdings will help them withstand unusual events happening in just one area or industry. It is especially important for people who want their investment portfolio to be balanced and able to cope well with risks.

Its steadiness largely supports people by reducing the psychological effects of risk in their investments. While markets are changing rapidly, investors sometimes make hurried choices to sell their assets. Stability in the market usually helps investors keep a cool head and stick to their main strategies. Reliable income from dividends is important to dividend investors who depend on it to achieve their personal goals.

In addition, a stable economy is supported by good market conditions. Because of this, businesses in generous countries are able to earn a stable income and, as a result, pay reliable dividends to shareholders. Businesses in an unchanging market can invest in new growth possibilities, which can help them give out higher dividends.

As a result, both companies and their investors enjoy increased benefits from each other.

To sum up, a stable market forms the basis for making dividend investing successful. It enables investors to create a strong portfolio equipped with reliability, balance, and stability in tough times. With stable markets, companies can give regular dividends to investors and maintain their income. As a result, market stability benefits the entire economy and leads to a partnership between investors and the markets they belong to. Investors need stable markets in order for dividend investing to be secure; thus, dividend investing shows how crucial it is to the economy.

Case Studies of Success

Reading outdoor stories of people who use dividend investing can show you how to be financially free. An example is the story of Sarah, who proves the importance of staying patient and investing balance after balance. At first, she started investing when she was in her early thirties, using money that was not much. She regularly purchased stocks that paid dividends and made sure her money was spread over many types of companies. She reinvested every dividend she got, which allowed her investment to grow steadily over the years. She managed to increase her portfolio to $500,000 by the age of fifty, making her able to count on a regular and lasting stream of earnings. This case underlines the strong effects of continuous reinvesting, as it eventually leads to important financial achievements.

Otherwise, stories can also revolve around understanding the issues around risky investments. The worthiness of a strong-yield energy business attracted an investor. First, the stock looked very promising, but difficulties in the energy industry forced the dividend to be severely reduced. It showed me why it is important to be careful when looking for high earnings. The investor found out that it's important to judge whether dividends will be paid out again and assess the risks within a sector. Hence, this case points out that it is important to look after both profitability and stability and to invest in various markets to avoid facing risks with just one company.

The third example is about companies that turn their fortunes during a downturn in the market. In the period of the 2020 pandemic-related market collapse, an investor saw her portfolio's worth go down. Instead of losing control, she chose to keep sound investments in strong dividend stocks. Her continued commitment to holding on was rewarded when the market recovered, and her portfolio amounted to the same value, which kept giving her an uninterrupted income. This case clearly shows that dividend investing stands strong during hard times and why having a long-term plan matters.

They encourage and also give us useful lessons we can apply. They stress how reinvesting, spreading investments, and keeping your cool during turbulence is very important. Tales about those who invest in dividends can teach aspiring investors how to make progress since financial independence becomes possible when you patiently follow the right steps and make the right investments.

Addressing Volatility Fears

No matter the situation in investing, volatility is always present and tends to make even the most experienced investors feel unsure and concerned. Amid all the market ups and downs, dividend investing clearly provides stability and shows investors how to react to fears of volatility.

Unpredictable and quick changes in the market usually cause investors to fear losing their investments. Due to this fear, people may dump their investments or change useful investment strategies without thinking carefully. Knowing the true benefits and toughness of dividend investments is the main way to deal with changes in the market. A company's profits are split into dividends, which come regularly to shareholders and remain steady even in bad market times. Because it eases the financial pressure, constant cash income enables investors not to panic and sell their assets at a loss.

Getting dividends in times when the market is falling does a lot to ease investors' worries. Receiving dividends helps you avoid worrying too much, as your income never changes, even when the stock market upsets do. Because of their consistent income, investors feel more confident and can stick to their decisions during hard times in the market.

Handling worries about volatility can be done by holding investments in different industries and regions. When they spread their funds into several different industries and parts of the world, investors can lower how much they depend on a single factor in the economy. Using this strategy, the risk is minimized, and the company can still make reliable returns when some areas do not perform well. You can also consider buying Dividend Aristocrats, as they have proven records of making regular dividend payments. These companies have regularly provided dividends and kept increasing them over many years, showing that they are financially strong and Stable during different economic periods.

In addition, including defensive sectors in their portfolio can be a good idea for investors. These three sectors are normally stable even when the economy goes through ups and downs. Industries are important because they ensure people and companies will always need their essential goods and services. When they invest in more of these sectors, investors can better safeguard their investment portfolios from market changes.

One more method is to save some funds aside so you can buy stocks for lower prices during market corrections. Thanks to bargain prices, investors can make good returns and keep believing in what they do, especially when others decide to act cautiously.

Basically, facing the risk of dividend changes in investing requires staying disciplined and patient. You should consider how dividend income will help you in the coming years and the difference compounding can have. If investors maintain different investments, put money into defensive sectors, and rely on cash savings, they can turn fluctuations in the market for their gain. By taking this approach, people can enjoy financial security as well as calmness as they keep working towards their financial goals.

Chapter 02: Debunking Dividend Myths

Not Just for Retirees

Some people think using dividends is meant only for those in retirement who need an additional regular payment. Even so, it should be noted that dividend investing brings benefits and options to people with any financial goals or levels of experience. In reality, including dividend investments can help create an investment portfolio that is strong and resistant to changes.

The main focus of dividend investing is that companies make regular payments to their shareholders. Usually, dividends are given from the company's earnings and may provide dependable income at any time. In any uncertain economy, dividends come in handy as they give investors some stability, apart from the stock itself going up in value.

A major reason why many people like dividend investing is that it allows for compounding. Reinvesting the money from dividends helps investors obtain more shares and, hence, collect bigger dividends. With time, this can make the investment portfolio's total returns much better. The idea of this compounding effect can be very useful for young investors since they have many years until they retire. The sooner dividends are reinvested, the higher the chances for big changes in wealth.

There is no reason why a person cannot do both dividend and growth investing at the same time. Numerous companies that offer dividends also have great opportunities for growth. These corporations are called Dividend Aristocrats because they have grown their dividends for many years, which suggests strong businesses and dedication to shareholders. With such firms, investors can get rewards from both dividends and an increase in the value of their shares.

Besides getting money for retirement, dividend investing may be suitable for other financial needs. People looking to save for the long run can depend on dividends to boost their portfolio's performance. A parent may earn dividends to cover tuition fees for the family, whereas some individuals might strive to retire early because of it. Because dividend investing is flexible, it can be applied to various goals a person may have.

Some people wrongly think that having a lot of money is needed to begin investing in dividends. Because of fractional shares and dividend reinvestment plans (DRIPs), investors can start with little money and enjoy the growing value of dividends. Dividend investing is suitable for both experienced and new investors since it helps everyone gain returns.

In the long run, dividend investing is a flexible way to enjoy financial security, feel secure, and experience growth. Mutual funds provide benefits to all who want to diversify their assets and are not just meant for people close to retirement. People who follow the principles of dividend investing are well-equipped to reach their financial targets in the long run.

Income vs. Growth Misconceptions

Many people wrongly view dividend investing as Having to choose between getting income and achieving growth. A lot of investors believe that dividend-focused portfolios won't grow while growth-focused ones won't earn much income. This kind of thought process can make people miss out on great opportunities and leave their investment sets unbalanced.

Dividend investing is suitable for people other than just retirees who want to earn immediately. Actually, this strategy is flexible enough to reach a range of aims, including current income, long-term growth, or a good balance between them. Many people think dividend stocks are uninteresting and do not earn much because they do not see how dividends contribute to the growth of an investment. From looking at historical data, stocks that provide dividends usually perform just as well or even better than those that do not across several years.

Dividend growth stocks stand out since they let investors earn a steady income and benefit from rising capital value. If a company consistently gives higher dividends, investors may be attracted by its stable finances and good growth prospects. Having a record of boosting dividends annually, these companies, called Dividend Aristocrats, suggest that including dividend growth should maybe be an area to consider for one's portfolio.

Investors ought to take into account that dividend strategies are quite flexible. A person's stage in life and their financial aims influence whether to focus on today's income, expand in the years ahead, or achieve a good balance. Contributors in their early careers could decide to use dividends to help with compound growth, while soon-to-be retirees tend to seek income to make sure they have enough money aside from their pensions. Therefore, dividend investing shows that people do not need to decide between income and growth; the strategy can be changed as financial needs progress.

This belief that dividend investments are safer than others is just another falsehood. Even though dividends can serve as a protection against market swings, each dividend stock has its qualities. People who invest in high-yield stocks should be careful since these dividends might not last and could eventually get cut. For this reason, one must understand the financial condition of a company and check if its dividends can be sustained over time.

All things considered, questions about the income-growth trade-off are usually founded on a false assumption. Since dividend investing offers different strategies, you can adjust your plan to accomplish your objectives and receive income. When these misconceptions are cleared, people can understand dividend investing well enough to use it to grow their wealth.

Challenging the Boring Label

Some people see dividend investing as boring and lacking excitement when it comes to investing. Yet, although this strategy is simple, it offers many opportunities that could change a portfolio into a strong and worthwhile investment. Often, new investors believe dividends are nothing exciting and prefer to look for fast-paced stocks that offer a bigger profit instead. If we look closely at dividend investing, it turns out to be a flexible choice that helps people reach several financial goals.

An argument against working out that dividends are boring comes from looking at the past performances of dividend-paying stocks. Over the years, companies that continue to award dividends and make them higher have given their shareholders regular income and provided higher accumulated results than other companies that do not distribute dividends. It is mainly because of how dividends are reinvested, which significantly adds to a portfolio's growth over the period. Even though dividend stocks tend to grow slowly, their ability to handle market downfall is what makes them attractive.

Besides, dividend investing adapts to each person's needs and can be customized at different stages of life. Today's young professionals can make the most of long-term benefits and increasing income by investing in dividend growth stocks. However, many retirees focus on high-yield stocks so they can keep getting a regular income. Due to their ability to change, investors can build portfolios that match their financial aims, whatever they may be.

Sometimes, distributing extra dividends can protect a company from the dangers of market uncertainty. In unfavorable economic conditions, dividends help investors receive steady income and avoid losing money by selling what they own right away. It is especially attractive to those people who want their money to be secure when the market changes.

What is more, dividend investing usually leads individuals to plan for the future and exercise financial caution. Focusing on steadily growing companies and careful decision-making becomes normal among investors. It helps you avoid risk and also increases the chance of steady results.

Even though dividend investing brings many benefits, many people misunderstand or do not understand it well. Some think that starting in this area demands a significant amount of capital and that the setbacks are less likely with dividend shares. Nevertheless, by being able to buy fractional shares and cheap brokerage fees, creating a dividend portfolio is now available to more people. It is also important to tell apart trusted payers from dividend stocks that could be at stake in reducing distribution.

To sum up, dividend investing challenges people who think investment must be boring because it is flexible and can bring many benefits. It gives people the chance to benefit from fixed income and also experience growth, creating a strong approach for handling many financial ambitions. When investors learn more about this strategy and its details, people will see that dividend investing is anything but boring.

Flexibility for Different Goals

Through dividend investing, an investor can meet several financial goals depending on whether they want immediate income, slow and steady growth, or something in between. Thanks to this flexibility, people are able to adjust their investments based on their current situation and what they wish to accomplish ahead. Those concerned with getting income quickly can use dividend stocks to increase what they earn from other investments. It suits people who want to work less so they can enjoy their lives. If investors choose high-yield dividend stocks, they can get regular payments that make the portfolio consistent with income.

With a longer time frame, younger investors or those with long-term investments usually concentrate on compound growth. Here, dividend reinvestment plans (DRIPs) prove to be a useful way, as they take the dividends and turn them into more shares of the stock. Doing so results in buying more shares in the company and helps the portfolio's value grow rapidly. Anyone focusing on rapid growth in their investments should pay special attention to companies that have regularly increased their dividends because this may lead to both better profits and greater dividends.

Individuals who want to earn and grow at the same time can choose a mixed investment method. One needs to choose stocks that pay high dividends and those that are likely to grow in market value. When you invest in various fields and places, it is possible to manage risks and gain from market growth without fullening your income. The relaxed nature of this investment strategy can be adapted to any person's ability to withstand risk and their financial ambitions.

A person's age and circumstances will affect the right approach to dividend investing. Beginning professionals prefer stocks whose value can rise, but as someone near retirement plans, income-producing stocks are more likely to be of interest. In the same way, those who retire often go for high-yield investments to make sure their capital stays intact.

One more benefit of dividend investing is that you can alter your investment plan when changes happen in your life. In case someone loses employment, gets an inheritance, or runs into expenses they did not expect, they are able to change their investment plan. Being flexible is beneficial in dividend investing since it helps people face unexpected events with ease and protect their retirement funds.

In the end, being able to choose how to invest with dividends draws a broad group of investors. Knowing what a person wants to accomplish financially and how much risk they can tolerate allows greater control in choosing an investment portfolio. Thanks to this flexibility, dividend investing is and will always be a useful and reliable method for reaching financial goals at any stage or when conditions change.

Chapter 03: Understanding Your Investment Profile

Identifying the Ideal Investor

Recognizing key traits of a good investor can affect someone's financial future. Anyone who thinks and acts like a dividend investor with suitable goals can be called a dividend investor regardless of age, income, or location. Usually, this kind of investor is patient, does not panic, and prefers investment opportunities with regular income and a strong chance for capital growth that dividend stocks can offer.

A smart investor in dividend stocks views the process with strategy, knowing that being patient and disciplined matters a lot. The individual is not drawn by the chance to make money fast; instead, they are loyal to the continuous and stable benefits offered by dividends. They are aware that reinvesting what they get from dividends can help their portfolio to increase in value as the years go by.

Besides, this investor spends time learning about the details of dividend stocks and the market as a whole. They are capable of looking at financial records, figuring out the payout ratio, and determining if a company's dividends can be maintained in the future. Thanks to this background, they can decide on investments that provide interesting returns and also have good qualities and potential for development.

Someone who follows the dividend strategy must be able to hold their ground when markets fluctuate. They realize that although markets change, the dividend income they receive can help them in tough economic times. They do not let small changes in the market disturb them; instead, they look at how their investments grow and earn money as time passes.

A good investor is also wise enough to center their investments in different industries and regions so risks do not burden them. Experienced investors realize that including growth-oriented dividend stocks in their portfolio alongside high-yield stocks is a better approach to making money in the long run.

This person takes note of the taxes involved and puts funds in tax-preferred accounts to increase their total earnings. They adjust their investment plans when there are changes in tax laws so that their investments give the best results.

In addition, the best investor changes their approach as their personal needs and goals in life shift. They keep reviewing their portfolio to match their long-term ambitions and change it when needed.

To sum up, the smart investor has two main goals: funding a comfortable retirement and ensuring needs for both him or herself and family members are taken care of. Through dividend investing, they establish a dependable income source for their goals and prove that it is a wise plan for building wealth slowly over time with the right attitude.

Setting Clear Financial Goals

Clear financial goals form the basis for the successful management of a dividend portfolio and the growth of your wealth. To sum up, being precise about these goals helps chart the path and ensures every investment fits into the investor's main financial goals.

The first thing to do is to look within and know your financial situation before making financial goals. Before making any decisions, investors have to properly look at their financial situation by focusing on income, expenses, debt, and assets. It makes it possible to select the resources you can use for dividend investing. Managers should not aim too high or too low when planning the activity for a preset timeframe.

Once the financial status is clear, the next thing to do is to specify clearly what you want to achieve. Each person's goals may be very different from those of another investor, based on their situation and what they hope to achieve. A few people try to get some extra income to handle monthly expenses, while others make long-term plans to save up for retirement or become financially free.

The goals should be Specific, Measurable, Achievable, Relevant, and defined in a particular time frame. Instead of creating a general goal to earn more dividend income, it would be better to have the SMART goal of making $10,000 in dividends annually within five years by investing in high-value companies that pay dividends. Targeting a certain area and setting a specific timeline allows for smoother tracking of progress and making updates whenever required.

It is also important to figure out your risk tolerance when making financial plans. Before picking dividend stocks, investors should think about their attitude toward risk and how much they can handle since this will help them decide the best strategies to use. Someone who follows conservative investing often looks for companies that offer consistent results and reliable income through dividends. Furthermore, an aggressive investor usually aims for larger returns, even if it means accepting more ups and downs.

A monitoring approach should be in place when dividend investors set their goals. It means holding reviews from time to time to see if goals are being achieved and making any required changes to the approach to investing. For example, you may need to look at your dividend stocks again, redistribute your assets if they did not perform well, or adjust to the recent changes in the market. Monitoring the progress of your investments guarantees that you meet your goals regardless of what happens in life or financial markets.

It is also very important to stay adaptable. People's financial goals should be updated when there are changes in their lives, finances, or preferences. Keeping their aims up-to-date and achievable is important, so investors should not be afraid to change them if needed. Because of this adaptability, investors can deal with uncertainties in the financial world and also be successful in dividend investing.

To finish, your financial aims should be made clear when you start investing in dividends. It gives guidance, assists with making choices, and is used to evaluate how well the company is doing. If investors choose a strategy that supports their set goals, they are more likely to do well in the financial markets and realize their financial goals.

Mindset for Success

It's very important to develop a winning mindset when you invest in dividends. Getting started means realizing that being patient is very important. The approach to dividend investing requires a person to plan for a long-term goal. With this approach, you ignore short-term changes and concentrate on the positive effects that regular earnings offer over the years. It means forecasting your investments' growth when you keep reinvesting your dividends and profit from the "compounding" process, which builds gradually but leads to a significant impact in the long run.

Having self-discipline is very important for this kind of mindset. Investors need to stick to their strategy for reaching their goals, not giving in to the urge to make quick profits. It is important in this discipline to avoid the exciting opportunities that can make you move away from your main strategy. Rather, a smart dividend investor doesn't change their chosen stocks so that time and persistent earning can take effect.

Considering the realities of a situation is very important. Dividend investing takes time and patience to create wealth; it cannot make anyone rich quickly. Being aware of this allows people to be happy as their wealth slowly increases. Thinking this way is necessary to remain upbeat and avoid disappointment when you don't experience results immediately.

Investors should always be ready to learn new things. Since the financial world is always developing, I should pay attention to changes in the market, key indicators, and company results. Regular learning helps investors know when to take action, how to manage their resources better, and how to watch out for any risks ahead.

Being resilient is necessary in the way people approach their chances of success. Things can never be known in advance in the market, and downturns will eventually happen. People who remain committed during downturns in the market usually understand that temporary drops can mean good chances to purchase. Risk is lowered, and the effects of market changes are reduced when a portfolio has lots of different types of investments.

It is important in a successful mindset to be sure about your financial objectives and how much risk you are able to take. People who invest should routinely check their investments and what they want to achieve from their investments to see if changes are needed. With this approach, you remain focused, and your plans fit well with your financial situation.

To do well in dividend investing, one needs patience, to follow rules, to have reasonable expectations, to learn often, to be strong, and to be consciously aware of one's goals. Following these rules, investors are able to deal with the uncertainties in the market and benefit from long-term growth and financial security thanks to dividend investing.

Common Misconceptions

Some false ideas about dividend investing can make new investors hesitant to make the most out of this type of investment. Some people think that only those with a substantial amount of money can start investing in dividends. Such a belief sometimes scares novice investors by making them think benefits are for those with extensive portfolios. In fact, even with limited resources, people can start assembling a dividend portfolio. Investors can buy fractional shares and make use of affordable brokerage to let their investments grow bit by bit throughout the years.

It is common for people to believe that since they receive dividends, their money is safe. Although dividends can provide you with regular income, some dividend-paying stocks are better than others. High-yield stocks tend to attract investors and may seem safe; still, many times, the dividends are not sustainable because the business is not strong. One needs to tell apart companies that have always paid dividends and stable fundamentals from those that offer high dividend yields to attract investors.

Divide investing can be tricky, and this fact often stops newcomers from trying. Most people find financial language and its rules to be rather overwhelming. However, the truth remains that having some support and interest can help anyone figure these topics out. First, it helps to concentrate on learning some basic things, and only after that do you move on to harder challenges. Numerous learning tools make things easier by breaking down the concepts and showing them with helpful graphics.

Many people often think that getting dividends means a stock is less risky than one that does not pay a dividend. Although some dividend-paying companies have survived for a long time and are sturdy, they cannot eliminate risks. Dividends should not always seem too good to be true, as often they might hide important problems. Working through the company's financial records and split information and checking whether the growth can be sustained helps investors measure the risk related to dividend stocks.

In addition, people question whether dividend investing is important in other nations. Certain individuals may agree that this form of investing is just for American stocks, but it also works well in the UK, Canada, and Australia. Since every market has specific features and tax rules, people who invest internationally must recognize the details of international dividend investing.

After looking at these misconceptions, it is obvious that dividend investing can be easily followed, customized, and used for different purposes. No matter if you aim to earn income now, in the future, or a mix, you should find a strategy that fits with what you want. After dismissing these myths, investors have a clear view and the ability to use dividend investing for their finances advantageously.

Chapter 04: Getting Started in Dividend Investing

Opening a Brokerage Account

To start with dividend investing, it is necessary to open a brokerage account first. This process is easy, but you still need to think through a number of decisions before you begin your investment journey. Choosing which brokerage firm to work with should be your first concern, especially if it fits your needs and desires. Because it matters, you should spend time finding out what is best to meet your needs. A decision can be made by checking if the firm is easy to use, helps with customer issues, and has special features for dividends.

The next step is to collect all the required papers so the account can be opened with ease. Normally, you will need to show personal details, including a driver's license or passport, proof of where you live, and your tax identification number. Beginning the process with collected documents makes the process easier and almost guarantees on-time transactions.

The process of creating an account is a bit different for residents of each country due to various country regulations. Those who live in the United States could deal with contrasting practices compared to those who live in the United Kingdom or Canada. Since this is the case, it requires a specific method that makes learning about country-specific details essential.

When starting a brokerage account, be sure to pick the account that fits your investment plan well. People have the option of regular taxable accounts or accounts with tax benefits like IRAs in the United States or ISAs in the United Kingdom. Every type of account offers different features and rules about how dividends are taxed. Being aware of these points can make a big difference to your profit from real estate.

When deciding on an account, also look at the payment methods that suit the way you handle your finances. Transferring part of your income from your main bank may encourage you to keep saving regularly. Since you choose to do this, your investments continue to grow steadily over time with less need for you to keep adjusting them.

Investors should be ready for typical obstacles that they could meet while signing up for an account. If there are problems with residency or responses are delayed, become aware of the policies at the brokerage and prepare well for each task. At times, people with dual citizenship or those living overseas can have additional issues, calling for a unique way of setting up their accounts.

Creating a list helps to avoid any complications when opening an account. Some things to have in mind during this process are confirming your personal information, learning about the brokerage's costs, and picking an account type that suits your investment objectives. Having completed these steps, opening a brokerage account is easy and makes dividend portfolio growth possible.

Choosing the Right Accounts

Deciding on the right accounts matters a lot for dividend investors who want to make money and reduce taxes. Deciding on the type of account can greatly change how much money you keep after paying taxes on your investments. Any investor trying to boost their portfolio strategically should first analyze the accounts offered in various countries.

First, you should become aware of the options, for example, taxable accounts, retirement accounts with tax benefits, and those abroad. The perfect fit for an investor varies depending on his or her situation and dreams. Although you can contribute to a taxable account as much as you want, your dividends are usually subject to yearly taxes. However, some countries like the US, UK, Canada, and Australia make it possible to either postpone or avoid tax altogether in accounts such as IRAs, ISAs, TFSAs, and Superannuation.

Investors need to recognize how taxation affects every type of account. Tax-advantaged accounts allow the income from your investments in the form of dividends to accumulate at a faster speed since the tax is either paid later or not at all. As an example, this situation is helpful when planning for the future since investments can earn more money by reinvesting, not by having to pay taxes every year. At the same time, these plans put limits on how much you can put in and how early you can withdraw your money.

Also, when you invest in other countries, there are extra concerns, including the taxes on foreign dividends and the process of understanding tax treaties. People who own international stocks should notice these matters and prepare well to pay less tax. For example, someone from the UK purchasing shares in US companies may have to use particular tax forms to receive back the withholding taxes or advantage from tax treaties.

Selecting an account type means connecting your goals with the features of the account. In some cases, putting high-yield stocks in tax-advantaged accounts is advisable to avoid immediate taxes on the income. In contrast, growth-oriented stocks might do better in taxable accounts since the tax rate on their gains is lower than usual incomes. Investors can rely on decision trees and checklists to find the best accounts, considering what they want to do with their money and their tax circumstances.

It helps a lot if your contributions are managed by the system and deposited at regular intervals. If money is automatically transferred from checking to investment, investors can follow their plans with little effort.

Choosing proper accounts is very important for a successful approach to dividend investing. It is necessary to clearly understand the tax system, match your goals with your account type, and continually continue to invest. Properly managing the selected accounts helps investors increase their finances and gradually develop a strong, profitable portfolio.

Initial Investment Strategies

At the start of investing in dividends, the strategy you use may strongly affect how your portfolio grows. Taking into account the main principles and what your goals are helps ensure your financial progress and income.

Before anything else, every investor should decide on their financial goals. Would you like to get quick profits, grow your wealth steadily in the future, or use both strategies? A clear understanding of these points makes it possible to build a strategy that is fitting for you. As an example, young investors want to make money from appreciation, knowing it will grow over time, whereas those close to retirement worry about earning enough money to meet their daily living expenses.

The selection of a suitable brokerage account is very important at the beginning. Depending on where you are, the kinds of options and their rules will affect your investments differently in the US, UK, Canada, and Australia. Saving in accounts such as IRAs, ISAs, or TFSAs helps you keep more of the returns since the dividend payments are not fully taxed.

While choosing stocks, put your emphasis on companies that have constantly paid dividends and have grown over the years. The process requires a look at key metrics such as the percentage of earnings as dividends, how stable those earnings are, and how much the firm's dividends have risen in the past. Firms that focus on giving out profits to shareholders and continue to be strong financially are accepted into most dividend portfolios.

Spreading investments in various sectors and parts of the world lessens risks. A portfolio with several different investments is safer from regional downturns and overall economic swings. Investing in both domestic and foreign dividend stocks may help protect income from local problems in the economy.

Selecting either stocks or dividend-paying ETFs is an important part of developing a portfolio. While individual stocks may bring higher profits and increased value, ETFs are diversified on their own and require less effort to study. Investors have to think about their willingness to do research and about how much time they will devote to their investment plan.

Deciding on how much money to invest is very important. Part of your decision is to decide how much of your portfolio to give to each stock, considering the gain you could get as well as the possible losses. Equal balance, dividing the funds into main and smaller parts, or making allocations based on risk may effectively assist with this aspect.

It is necessary to plan regular contributions and reinvestment into the portfolio. DRIPs make it easy for shareholders to reinvest their dividends automatically for more compounding effects. Planning frequent investments steadily allows your money to grow as it benefits from dollar-cost averaging to absorb changes in the market.

To sum up, being well-prepared and making good decisions at the start lays a good path for profitable dividend investing. Making portfolios fit with personal plans, spreading investments in various areas, and having a savings plan every year make a portfolio stronger and fit to contribute to growth and earnings.

Avoiding Get-Rich-Quick Schemes

Being successful in dividend investing means ignoring the urge to make a fast profit. It is necessary to realize that this strategy does not promise overnight wealth but delivers slow and stable growth. Understanding that making quick and larger profits usually involves a lot of risk is especially important in this field. Being told that dividends can help you make a large gain overnight is a warning that should be noticed.

People who invest should understand that good returns take time to materialize. Earning meaningful income from dividends takes a long time, as it does not happen overnight. In the start, things may take a while, though regular reinvestment leads to bigger achievements. For example, starting with a small sum can help your portfolio expand a lot during the next two decades if the dividends are reinvested.

Having patience is one of the most important parts of successful dividend investing. It is important to realize that the growth caused by earnings creating more earnings takes time to develop. Slowly investing some money over time often leads to good results in the future. Receiving your first dividend may make you feel more encouraged than following the changing values of the market every day.

Paying attention to how your investment process works rather than the first results will help you avoid changing your plan. Noticing every little gain and remembering that every dividend received is part of the larger plan can lessen the worry caused by short-term changes in the market. Thinking about the process instead of just the result improves the way people handle their investments.

An experienced investor stays alert to any offer involving unrealistic returns. Thanks to these promises, people might overlook the risks that can cause them to lose their money. Investors should focus on slow, lasting growth and choose sound investments rather than pursue great returns.

Dividend investing ultimately depends on having a disciplined style and looking for moderate success instead of taking big risks. Following these guidelines, investors ensure they have a strong financial outlook and get reliable income from their dividends. Even though building wealth takes a certain amount of time, this course can help you manage your money in a steady and long-lasting fashion.

Chapter 05: Building a Diversified Portfolio

The Importance of Diversification

Having different kinds of investments helps protect from the uncertainty found in the markets. Spreading your investments into various assets is the main idea behind diversification to avoid being vulnerable to one kind of risk. Dividend investing most often requires going about it this way to build a reliable and steady income stream.

Diversification mainly helps you reduce your risks. The practice of dispersing investments in different areas helps to lessen the impact of risk in any particular section of the market. If an investor concentrates too much of their portfolio on technology or energy, it can suffer from those sectors' changes in the market. On the other hand, a diversified portfolio helps reduce the effects of bad events occurring in any single area due to holding different investments.

In addition, using a variety of geographic locations adds extra safety. The way a country's economy, politics, and currency move can be highly different when reviewing other nations. Purchasing both domestic and global dividend stocks or funds allows investors to reduce the risks from their markets, so their earnings keep going even when times are tough locally.

Having different sources of income helps you cope with income changes. A company can decide on dividend cuts at any time because of its problems or because of a general slowdown in the economy. Owning several companies that give dividends helps investors weather the effects of less income from a single stock. Using this approach, the total income from the portfolio usually does not change much, even if some of the investments have troubles.

Diversification does not only control risks; it can even lead to better returns. Although diversification is mostly known for protecting investments, it helps investors to benefit from growth elsewhere and in other markets. A wide mix of investments can give investors profit due to the changing cycles in various industries and countries. Having a wide range of investments raises the possibility of having assets that do well and promote the growth of your portfolio.

Having several kinds of holdings in a portfolio is also an aspect of diversification. Even with a large number of stocks in your portfolio, you need to be sure it remains easy to handle. Having excess investments may make it difficult to watch over and manage the portfolio well. Consequently, investors need to choose a number of stocks that offer a decent spread and remain practical.

To get real diversification, you must carefully plan and check your portfolio from time to time. People should check their portfolios at regular intervals to see if the mix of investments is good for their level of risk and what they wish to achieve. At any stage, it is important to modify investments to keep up with new market developments and changing personal needs.

All in all, being diversified is a basic rule for those interested in dividend investing. It results in less risk, more stable earnings, and the chance for higher returns if investments are shared among different sectors, areas, and types of assets. Diversifying investments helps portfolios withstand the difficulties that usually appear in financial markets.

Global Diversification

One of the main things to do in dividend investing to manage risks and increase profits is to have holdings worldwide. It consists of investing in many countries, which shields portfolios from shaky markets and allows the fund to benefit from interesting investments elsewhere.

There is a common interest among investors to invest in the countries they are familiar with because they believe it is safer. Having this home bias can prevent you from making use of opportunities in other successful economies. Allowing investments in different countries gives investors more opportunities to use changes in other nations' economies, currencies, and industry sectors. This scheme works well when the country's economy is not doing well or when the domestic market struggles.

Being diversified internationally helps investors face dangers such as political problems, recessions, or new laws from different countries. Sometimes, a country's economy may slow down, while in another country, things are booming, helping to stabilize returns at the portfolio level. Besides, some countries may offer special resources or industries that you won't find much in your home country.

Commonly, investors add international diversity to their dividend portfolio by buying foreign stocks or ETFs that pay out dividends. With these tools, the portfolio can access several markets, making it more steady over time. Such countries as Canada, the UK, and Australia are particularly known for their major dividend-providing businesses, so investors find them interesting for investing overseas.

Nevertheless, making investments in other countries comes with issues related to different currencies and tax rules. The currency exchange rate might modify the amount of dividends the investor can take home. In order to avoid potential losses, investors should know about these risks and either hedge or pick investments made in stable currencies.

Taxation is an important point, too, since foreign dividends may need to pay withholding taxes in the nation where the company is located. It's a good idea for investors to study tax treaties and decide whether their investments can be placed in tax-advantaged accounts to improve after-tax profits.

Successful diversity across the world calls for investors to include both domestic and international assets in their holdings. It can be achieved by picking the right stocks and ETFs while considering their segment allocation, payment of dividends, and prospects for growth. Taking care of a variety of holdings means routinely monitoring and fixing the amounts invested to fit with the market and your own financial goals.

To sum up, spreading investments worldwide is a useful way for dividend investors to improve their results and reduce risks. Welcoming more options in their investments can help investors gain from opportunities worldwide and potentially get higher and more secure payouts. Strategic planning and smart choices when going global help make dividend investing solid for long-term results in the world.

Position Sizing

Finding out how much to invest in each company's stock is key to doing well as a dividend investor. How much investment you put into each stock is important for controlling risks and avoiding one stock overpowering the rest. Thinking about how much they should invest in each asset, people can spare their portfolios from serious losses and unlock their potential.

What defines position sizing most is that it helps you cut down on risks. You should not invest too much in just one stock since this could lead to big losses if the stock does poorly or lowers its dividends. In this situation, an investor would notice a big cut in income if the company reduces or cancels its dividends, which make up such a big portion of the portfolio. As a result, it is important to have a proper mix of various kinds of holdings to keep your portfolio steady.

Equal weighting is one of the most basic ways to set up your portfolio, with every stock taking up the same percentage. By using this way, no one investment can overly influence the portfolio, so it is easy to spread the risks and keep things simple. At the same time, equal weighting is straightforward and works well, but it may sometimes be different from what an investor needs.

In addition, risks can be considered when determining how much money to invest in each security. Knowing the reliability of a company's dividend and how volatile the stock is, investors can decide how much they will invest in every company. When using this method, more details are needed for each stock, yet the outcome is a portfolio that matches the investor's risk preferences.

Those who want to get the best of both strategies can try the core-satellite method. Using this approach, a larger amount of assets is put into steady investments, and a little is kept in more unpredictable or riskier companies. Investors get to take part in the strong growth of risky investments and still rely on dependable dividends from their safer companies.

Dealing with the stocks that make up the larger share is something that needs careful thought. Stable companies that have given regular dividends and are financially sound are what most core holdings consist of. Gaining a higher exposure to these stocks could take place because many view them as more stable and with a steady financial stream. In other situations, satellite positions involve companies with the possibility of high growth but also bigger risks, so investors may put less money into them to protect themselves.

Analysts and investors make the calculating process easier by using step-by-step sheets or online position sizing calculators. They help determine the ideal sum to invest after checking the investor's risk level and the goals of the portfolio. After filling in details such as their preferred diversification and the level of risk in each kind of stock, investors are better able to decide how much of an investment to make in each one.

To sum up, using proper position sizing is the main way to manage risk when you invest in dividend stocks. Investors can determine how to manage their money by turning to equal weighting, a risk-based sharing approach, or a combination of what they believe is safe and volatile. Having a disciplined approach saves you from losses and also makes it likely that you'll receive dependable income from your investments.

Balancing Yield and Growth

Being successful in dividend investing means you need to weigh the risks and chances of gaining money. There is a common choice for investors, whether to pick stocks that pay right away or those with greater growth prospects later on. Rather than picking one type of investment, people should combine them in a way that ties to their financial goals and how much risk they can handle.

Retirees and individuals who want to earn regular income appreciate high-yield dividend stocks since they offer fast returns. Many of these stocks come from companies working in stable and traditional fields, which are organized so they can give investors a big chunk of their profits as dividends. Even so, sometimes, people miss the possible risks while looking for promising yields. Handing out very high dividends instead of investing in the company's future may create problems in the long run.

Most often, companies in hot sectors like technology and healthcare are the ones with the fastest-growing dividends. Although these companies pay out small dividends at first, their yield can increase a lot over the years as the corporation grows. Because of this growth, you could receive capital appreciation, which makes up a big part of your total returns. Although growing stocks do not pay dividends as soon as high-yield stocks can, their ability to increase payouts can bring in a lot of money in time.

A person's financial situation and ambitions should be looked at before choosing the right balance between yield and growth. If a young investment is for the long run, emphasizing growth can let dividends accumulate through the years. In contrast, when they are about to retire, many investors prefer to look at yield to make sure they get a steady income. Factors you should pay attention to are the stage your life is in, the amount you need to live on, and how willing you are to take risks.

Various model portfolio blends allow investors to match their goals and risk tolerance as their lives and risks change. If the goal of the portfolio is "Income Now," it will likely contain many high-yield stocks to supply today's income. With this type of portfolio, the main priority is finding stocks with growth potential in the future. It tries to find a balance by including stocks that earn a lot and keep investing in the future.

Some investor's common move is to focus on getting high dividends but not to be certain whether these dividends will be sustainable over the years. Having a higher dividend may seem like a good idea, but if the company cannot increase its payments, you may end up facing financial problems. Thoroughly check payout ratios, earnings, and the state of the industry to guarantee that the company's dividends will not stop.

What makes dividend investing successful is finding a place that suits your goals and willingness to take risks. Ensuring that you have enough yield and growth can give your portfolio stability and ensure it provides some cash while helping it grow for future gains.

Chapter 06: Choosing the Right Stocks

Identifying Blue-Chip Stocks

In this investment field, blue-chip stocks are recognized for being strong and providing assurance as well as stable growth. Their large market worth, familiar name, and stable practice of giving out dividends define such companies. Investors like blue-chip stocks because they manage to perform well and keep delivering returns whenever the economy is weak.

The main features of blue-chip stocks come from their strong financial and operational strength. On average, these organizations have a long background of making profits and are known as pioneers in what they do. Thanks to their many products or services, they are able to maintain revenue when faced with different market situations. In addition, well-known blue-chip brands tend to attract and retain a loyal customer base and support their business growth.

These companies are identifiable by their low levels of debt and by having good amounts of cash. As a result of their strong financials, they are able to continue increasing what they give shareholders in spite of economic obstacles. A record of growing dividends proves that the company is dedicated to rewarding its shareholders, which is important for investors who like dividends.

Most of the blue-chip stocks come from the consumer goods, healthcare, financial services, and technology industries. Since they remain stable and in high demand, the industries supporting blue-chip stocks are not easily moved by changes in the market. Johnson and Johnson and Procter and Gamble, both famous for a wide range of products, show how blue-chip stocks are reliable and strong.

Despite how attractive blue-chip stocks are, potential investors should know what their flaws are. Large corporations may have less impressive growth possibilities than younger and more flexible companies. This happens mainly because they are already very well established, which often impedes quick growth. Blue-chip stocks also experience market swings, and because they are large, they sometimes come under extra government supervision and pressure from other companies.

Even though there are problems, blue-chip stocks are still appreciated by dividend investors for their steady income and slight growth. Investors consider them as a good foundation since they reward with regular dividends and may see their value improve over time.

All in all, looking for blue-chip stocks requires understanding a company's situation in the market, how financially secure it is, and its history of paying dividends. Finding companies with steady performance and past achievements allows investors to put together a portfolio that copes with swings in the market and rewards them later on. Blue-chip stocks are important tools that any dividend investor should keep in their portfolio.

Navigating Dividend Aristocrats

The phrase 'Dividend Aristocrats' in dividend investing tends to make one think of stability and ongoing reliability of returns. These companies are special because they have, through decades, provided regular dividends to their shareholders. Any company hoping to be a Dividend Aristocrat needs to boost its dividend payment for at least 25 years straight. Such results are proof that their businesses work well, their income stands strong, and they are managed wisely.

A lot of investors choose to hold Dividend Aristocrats in their portfolio since these stocks are reliable and offer potential growth. Usually, these companies are large-cap, and they work in several fields, allowing investors to spread their risks in the market. What attracts people is that they can survive economic changes and still give returns to their shareholders. For a long time, Dividend Aristocrats have proven that they can protect what investors have while increasing the income received year after year.

Their strong performance in the past adds more attraction to Dividend Aristocrats. Studies indicate that these stocks usually do better than average over the years, helping investors gain from returns and regular income. The fact that the company can raise dividends every year is often because of how strictly it controls its finances. Firms in this group are usually known for having high cash flow, reasonable debts, and a strategy to grow steadily in the future.

Even so, investing in Dividend Aristocrats requires awareness of some problems. These well-established corporations may not be unaffected by the fluctuations in the economy. To reduce their investment risks, investors need to keep an eye on the companies' finances and changing trends in the market. Issues like lower revenue, more rival companies, and risks related to their industries can recoil on their promise to increase dividends year by year.

It is important to have a plan when you include Dividend Aristocrats in your portfolio. People who invest should make sure their money is placed in various industries and countries so they are not affected by one sector's misfortunes. It is also vital to check the payout ratio of every company as it helps forecast the dividend security. If a company has a high payout ratio, it might be trying to do too much and could stop increasing its dividend payments.

Dividend Aristocrats are good for new investors as they are less risky compared to other stocks. The steady rise in dividends that these companies have shown gives conservative investors a sense of reliability. Besides, having a place in this group increases the company's reputation, which shows the market that it is well-managed and will exist in the long run.

Overall, dealing with Dividend Aristocrats needs you to be diligent and think ahead. However, these companies cannot escape the general effects that happen in the economy. At every step, investors must be active, checking that their gathered assets communicate their risk factors and financial ambitions. Thanks to this approach, they gain from Dividend Aristocrats' power and work towards a satisfying investment process.

Avoiding Dividend Traps

Many times, people who focus on high-yield stocks are not aware of the risks these investments bring. Realizing the danger these traps pose and knowing how to skip them is very important for a profitable dividend portfolio. Granting a fantasy appeal is the main risk in dividend investing as a result of stocks that offer an average yield. Investors may end up in trouble financially when the company cannot pay its promised dividends.

You should first be able to see the signs that indicate a company's dividend could be unsustainable. Having a high dividend yield may, at times, signal a problem rather than a chance to invest. A decreasing stock price could be the reason for this yield, showing that the business is facing obstacles. Investors might consider avoiding companies that are losing revenue, have low free cash flow, or haven't been able to pay similar dividends. Because of these reasons, the company could have fewer or no dividends paid in the future.

Besides, checking the payout ratio is very important. By dividing the dividends by net income, we find out what percentage of the company's earnings is paid to shareholders as dividends. Payout ratios over 100% highlight that the dividends paid are larger than what the company earns, which cannot last for a long time. It is wise for investors to look for companies with conservative payout ratios since, this way, the business has extra earnings to help it expand and resist adverse economic conditions.

Diversification also goes a long way in avoiding possible trap decisions. Contributing money to a variety of industries and locations allows investors to handle risks more efficiently. It minimizes the damage of a cut in dividends and adds to the general stability of the portfolio. Because of their stable earnings and dividends, blue-chip stocks should be worth considering as part of your investment plans.

It is important to look at different resources to confirm that a company can continue paying dividends regularly. Investors should use company reports but also make use of what experts say, news, and developing tendencies in the industry. With this method, a person can see the overall financial situation of a company as well as its likelihood to pay dividends.

Setting certain requirements before including a stock in your portfolio may help avoid dividend traps. You should check for a suitable payout ratio, a rise in yields, and the company's solid financial standing to find a stock that meets your risk level and aims. As a result of following these rules, investors stay away from investing in projects that offer surprisingly high returns.

All in all, even though high returns look tempting, dividend investors should always remain carefully informed. Investors can defend themselves from fake dividends and obtain reliable earnings by paying attention to warnings, investing in different assets, and using clear standards for investing.

Evaluating Financial Health

It is important to look at the financial state when investing in dividends so you can be sure about the company's dividend payments. The Dividend Safety Scorecard makes it fast for investors to assess how financially sound companies are. Since the tool relies on colors, it is easy for anyone to interpret and select the best stocks for their needs.

Important financial measures are highlighted on the scorecard as they help answer questions about a company's financial condition. Of all, the payout ratio plays a key role in analyzing dividends. It points out how much of earnings is being sent out as dividends. When a company keeps very few earnings for business growth and returns too much to shareholders, it could negatively impact the company's growth potential. On the other hand, a lower debt-to-EBITDA ratio shows the company is handling its finances conservatively and could handle the downturns without needing big cash injections.

Another important factor to look at is how much the company's earnings are increasing. A rising yearly profit shows that a company may be able to keep giving out higher dividends. This growth is a sign that the company is running smoothly and also earning profits. Investors would do well to choose businesses whose earnings are consistently going up.

A major factor in the scorecard is also checking the debt-to-equity ratio. It offers information regarding the sources of funding the company uses for its operations. If a company's debt-to-equity ratio is high, it suggests it is using a lot of debt, and this may cause trouble in making future dividend payments if it faces financial difficulties. On the contrary, a lower ratio means a company gets most of its cash from its equity and not from taking on debt, which is usually considered risk-free and steady.

Checking the cash flow is just as necessary for assessing the financial position of a company. It provides a company with money to settle its bills and help with its future expansion. Having enough steady cash flow means a company can distribute dividends with ease. A complete analysis should be done to ensure that sufficient cash remains and to avoid any future cuts in dividends.

Viewing the company's history of paying dividends shows how keen it is to reward its shareholders. Companies with years of paying dividends, especially those that continue to increase them, usually show their success and commitment to shareholders. Still, swift dividend reductions or numerous cuts might signal that something is wrong with the business.

The use of these metrics in an overall review enables investors to get a clear idea of how steady a company's finances are. It is meant to support the process of assessing important holdings often and, therefore, reduce risks within the portfolio. Applying this method all the time allows investors to keep a close eye on their investments and choose dependable companies for their portfolios.

Such evaluations help avoid possible mistakes and make the investor feel that their portfolio is well-protected. Gaining knowledge and watching the financial status of their investments allows investors to act wisely and achieve better results from dividend investing.

Chapter 07: Advanced Portfolio Management

Portfolio Rebalancing

The art and science of keeping a proper balance in a portfolio are both required in dividend investing. Portfolio rebalancing involves checking and adjusting investments to see if they still fit with a person's money goals and attitude to risks. Taking on this routine ensures that the asset mix keeps supporting the original plan as other aspects change.

It's basically about fine-tuning an investment portfolio to keep the balance between risk and reward. If there are changes in the market, the initial balance may be altered because asset values change. In such a case, a portfolio that was equally divided between stocks and bonds could turn into a collection mainly made up of stocks if stocks do better than bonds. As a result of this trend, the risk in the portfolio could go up because stocks are riskier than bonds. Therefore, rebalancing is used to fix the allocation of assets and make it the way it is intended.

There are many positive outcomes from routinely rebalancing a portfolio. It supports risk management by ensuring that investing goes in line with the investor's ability to take risks. In addition, it allows investors to profit more by regularly buying investments when they are low and selling when they have increased. Here, poorly performing things get extra attention, and the overperforming ones are reduced, seeking to take advantage of the market's mistakes.

It is possible to find several approaches for rebalancing a portfolio. Sometimes, portfolios are rebalanced at regular points on a calendar, such as each quarter or each year. Even though this process offers predictability, its results might not always match the current market. Another method is to carry out rebalancing when there is a particular percentage difference in the weight of each asset compared to its target. The method reacts to changes in the market, not by following a regular timetable. Demand-based rebalancing is another option since it relies on incoming or outgoing cash to rebalance the portfolio, so you don't need to sell stocks or other assets.

Still, when rebalancing, one should be careful not to overtrade since this can cause new expenses and taxes. Anyone who invests should make sure to create rules and stick by them. In some cases, they could decide to rebalance once an asset's holding is more than 5% away from its goal or choose to look over their portfolio every year.

Besides, the process of rebalancing should suit each person's portfolio, taking into account when funds are likely to be used, any possible taxes, and transaction fees. For example, investments in IRAs are free from capital gains taxes when things are rebalanced, unlike when you hold securities in taxable accounts.

Portfolio rebalancing is different for every individual. It needs a plan that thinks about the investor's plans and the ever-changing market. Regularly rebalancing their investments according to a planned strategy allows investors to control risks and move closer to their key financial goals with dividend investing.

Managing Risk

When investing in dividends, taking care of your risk helps you support the health of your portfolio in the future. When a company reduces the amount of dividends it offers, it often takes investors by surprise. However, handling such a situation firmly and step-by-step can reduce risks and allow room for new avenues.

The first thing to do after a dividend cut is to find out more about the details and discover why the decision to reduce them was taken. It matters to look into the financial standing of the company thoroughly. One has to examine the financial statements to discover if the poor results are just a short-term challenge or suggest a long-term problem. They should pay attention to things such as decreasing sales, more debt, or circumstances in the market that may affect the company's earnings.

When the cause is clear, investors should decide if they should keep, sell, or change the stock they hold. Among the factors to think about is how this decision will change the overall yield, create tax obligations, and leave unrealized gains if another better choice is ignored. In particular, if many companies in the industry are lowering their dividends, it could be smart to reconsider the reliability of the sector.

Learning from real-life problems can be very helpful. There are times when keeping a stock after it cuts its dividend, which has resulted in even further losses for the investor due to the company's money problems. In some cases, stocks gained value strongly after a quick cut, which rewarded people who kept their faith in them. This means that companies should look at their situation rather than only following the industry's trends.

Another important task in handling risk is to rebalance the portfolio. After their dividends are cut, shareholders need to think about regaining the income they've missed. People may rebuild their income by taking advantage of DRIPs or transferring their money to steadier or more profitable investments. Securely choosing other stocks or investments allows investors to feel confident and keep enjoying regular income.

You should also continue to assess your portfolio periodically, besides responding to reduced dividends. It is important for investors to occasionally check their investments to make sure they are in line with what they want and can handle financially. If possible problems are found early, adjustments to the strategy can be made in a timely way.

Using various types of investments is one of the surest ways to handle risk. Dividing investments into different industrial and regional areas helps investors lower the risk caused by negative events occurring in a single place. To sum up, diversifying your portfolio helps you handle shifts in the market and gives you a steady income.

The goal in managing risk when you invest in dividends is to get income but keep your savings intact, too. Being aware of what's happening, using data to decide, and being adaptable in their approach, investors can find more confidence and security while investing in dividends. This way of investing helps people guard against potential losses and – at the same time – use new opportunities that arise in the financial world.

Tax Optimization

To get the best results from your dividend investments, you must handle the difficulties of tax optimization. If you consider the details of tax rules, you can increase the amount of income you receive from your dividend portfolio. To minimize what you pay in taxes, your assets are placed in different accounts and regions to ensure you get the highest net profit.

In tax optimization, it is important to know the different ways dividends are treated in each country. For example, qualified dividends are taxed at a lower rate than regular income in the United States, and this is very helpful for those investors in higher tax brackets. To enjoy this preferential tax status, you have to fulfill specific requirements, proving that planning your investments is very important.

Yet, in the United Kingdom, there is a dividend allowance that helps people receive up to a certain amount of dividends without having to pay taxes. In addition to this, the tax rate on your dividends will depend on your earnings. If you learn about these limits and allowances, you can invest your money wisely and have more of it remain in your pocket.

In Canada, the dividend tax credit reduces the tax that domestic investors have to pay on eligible stock dividends. It serves to include the taxes firms have already paid at the corporate level, which in turn helps avoid paying taxes several times. When Canadian investors use this system well, their tax situation can greatly improve.

People who own international shares should learn about withholding taxes. Such taxes are subtracted from dividends provided by foreign companies following the agreements in place between countries. Going through these treaties and choosing how to save on taxes with credits can keep your returns from decreasing over time. A U.S. resident, for example, can claim a foreign income tax credit by filling in Form 1116, even though this can be tricky to complete.

Taking time to choose which type of account is right for your dividend stocks might be important for your taxes. Money in these accounts is normally sheltered from immediate taxes, so your dividends can grow year after year. At the same time, each plan offers certain limits on your earnings and withdrawals, so following these rules allows you to skip any penalties.

It is also essential to know about "tax drag" to realize how taxes impact the growth of your investments. When assets are not placed wisely, you may end up paying more taxes on your dividends, which affects the gain and slows down growth in your investments. ==Looking at how different tax rates affect compound interest shows it is important to arrange your assets wisely.

To sum up, no single approach to tax optimization fits everyone when it comes to investing in dividend companies. You should work with a personalized plan that fits your details, including the country you live in, your earnings, and what you want to achieve in the future. Besides, if you monitor your portfolio and stay active, you can observe better results and ensure more savings for your future.

Handling Market Downturns

During a market fall, it is necessary to think strategically and use an organized approach to investments. During such moments, it's more important to look after one's portfolio instead of merely following how the market changes. Ensuring the portfolio has enough liquidity and will not easily break when there is volatility should be the main concern for investors.

Diversification plays an important role in managing risk, and it is very important to follow this strategy. Investors can defend their investments by owning different kinds of assets and a variety of sectors. For this reason, adding more exposure to sectors like consumer staples and utilities, which fare well in tough times, can shield your portfolio from other unpredictable sectors. Because of what they offer, these industries are always needed, and demand stays constant in any economic environment.

Having access to reserve funds is very important, too. Because they have this pile of cash, investors are able to take part in buying stocks when prices are low. It gives you some cash on hand to pay for unexpected costs so you can keep your investments intact.

Investors can improve the resilience of their portfolios by checking their investments' performance during various recession situations. An analysis of payout ratios, debts, and dividend records is required so that the companies in the portfolio can continue paying dividends even when the economy is slow. Having insight into the past shows that dividends often give companies protection during hard market conditions and recessions such as the 2008–2009 financial crisis.

Handling your emotions is very important during situations of decline. Volatility in the markets usually results in people feeling nervous and selling quickly, which can result in major losses. Pausing for one full day before making a selling decision can assist people so they don't react in the moment to market fluctuations. Options such as DRIPs and planned buys assist in letting investors continue their investment plans in spite of noisy markets.

Reading about long-lasting investors who have gone through market drops helps and motivates us. These investors tend to look at the slow growth of dividends instead of worrying about quick changes in stock prices. It's been noted by many that, by persevering through down markets, investors saw their dividend income rise in the future.

To deal with times of market downturns, one should depend on smart strategies, keep calm emotions, and think about long-term achievements. Following these rules allows dividend investors to safeguard their investments and be well-placed to succeed when markets are doing well again. Thanks to this approach, having a clear route to financial security and growth is reliable even in any market situation.

Chapter 08: Monitoring and Adjusting Your Portfolio

Using Alerts and Watchlists

Being attentive helps you ensure and boost the growth of your dividend portfolio. A simple technique to stay cautious is with the help of alerts and watchlists. Thanks to these tools, investors can monitor major occurrences that could shape their investments and be ready to make smart choice's.

Any sensible investor should make sure to set up alerts before anything else. Alerts can help you by informing you of critical events, including ex-dividend dates and any major changes to paying out dividends or main news impacting the company's shares. For example, people use Seeking Alpha and Yahoo! Features, which are included in finance that keep investors informed in real time about their holdings. Because of this, investors are well informed when sudden changes that affect dividends occur.

A watchlist, on the contrary, includes stocks an investor wants to keep an eye on for chances to buy or sell. When a watchlist is well organized, investors are able to review their existing stock and check out new options often. It helps investors look at the market and company performance in detail before deciding on any action.

Receiving alerts can highlight the first signs of any problems within a person's investments. Those who invest can register for alerts to learn when an important occurrence happens, such as a big cut in dividends or unexpected negative profit results. When a company's payout ratio gets above 80%, it can mean there are financial problems, so this warrants further investigation. If these signals are spotted in time, investors can prevent major losses from taking place.

It's also necessary to ignore unimportant information and pay attention only to the key facts. It is not always necessary to react immediately to alerts since minor changes might only cause stress and poor judgment. Investors need to distinguish regular market noise from true signs of trouble, so they only respond to alerts that indicate big changes in their portfolio's financial condition.

In general, managing a dividend portfolio effectively is made easier by making use of alerts and watchlists. These tools help investors follow the market, act fast with accurate data, and thus improve their chances of fulfilling their financial goals. When they use these strategies in their investment decisions, investors are able to act quickly and use new chances as they appear.

Tracking Dividend Income

When looking at dividend investing, investors must closely monitor their earnings since it helps them take action for the sake of their portfolios. Preparing requires frequent monitoring of dividends since they can tell you about your present finances and assist you in making better decisions in the future.

You should start by developing a reliable system that covers all the details of your dividend income. This step suggests jotting down the name of the company, the dividend amount, and the date when a payout is received. Such records are essential as they show the cash flow and help to see how the business's income remains steady as the years go by.

In addition, following the progress of dividend growth holds the same value as tracking income. Checking the rate of dividend increases allows you to see how well the company will perform in the future. Any changes to the number of dividends, however small, should be recorded regularly in an investor's records, and these records should be looked at to check the general well-being and outlook of their shares.

A great number of investors rely on digital support to track their funds properly. Some of these tools are easy spreadsheets, and others are advanced finance programs, depending on what you want to use them for. Investors should be able to use a template that helps them add data effortlessly and shows the total return, how fast it has increased, and how much yield they earn from it.

Automated systems are very important in tracking modern dividends. With alerts, investors do not miss important announcements about payments, dividend rewards, and transformations in a company's policies. Such alerts let investors act in a timely manner, whether they want to use their dividends or move their assets to better choices.

On top of that, using colors and automated tools makes it simpler to find any changes or unusual patterns in the data. So, when dividends are cut or the company's earnings unexpectedly change, colorful warnings in the app allow investors to act quickly and find out why.

It is strategic to keep track of set income levels since it keeps investors inspired and helps them keep moving toward their goals. If a person relies on dividend cash flow to pay for their monthly utilities, this shows that investing in dividends is helpful and rewarding in the long run.

In addition, yield and growth rates should be watched via the templates so farmers receive useful ideas for action. Investors may rely on these details to see how their portfolio meets their needs, making needed changes to improve their achievements.

Tracking dividend income helps you keep a full understanding of your financial situation, not only keeping records of the income. If investors track their finances well and make use of the latest tools, their dividend portfolios should be both safe and successful for many years.

Setting Income Milestones

Making targets for your income helps you plan how to reach your financial objectives when you invest in dividends. By choosing exact objectives, investors manage to make dividend earnings growth less overwhelming through steady progress. With this approach, you can enjoy coaching and follow clear signs of how much you have advanced.

The first thing you need to do is to figure out your main financial goal. It may mean using some of your income for retirement, for budgeting, or for paying for monthly utility costs or trips you make every year. After deciding on the main goal, the long-term aim can be divided into several small but important short-term aims. Such smaller targets help keep you inspired and happy as you reach each one.

So, an investor may pick a first goal of earning $100 in yearly dividends. As soon as this target is hit, you could work toward saving $500 and then $1,000 and grow from there. Every achievement helps boost confidence and confirms the investor's dedication to the dividend approach. Charts or graphs can be very helpful when it comes to checking these milestones since they clearly show the progress being made.

Hitting important income goals is another important part of this strategy. Giving credit and rewards when people do well encourage them and motivates them to continue improving. Spending some time together by going out for a meal or discussing your victories with other members of online investor groups is a good way to thank yourself.

Relating your dividend income to your life goals makes the process of investing more important. When linking major targets in life—for example, paying for a child's education, traveling to an amazing place, or retiring securely—investors keep themselves closely connected to their finances and find motivation.

Goal setting based on income also urges people to handle their investments better. This means that investments have to be reviewed regularly, and the portfolio could be changed to keep moving toward every goal. So investors stay clear about changing their plans or looking for fast or high-risk opportunities.

All in all, having income milestones makes achieving financial independence something real and possible for most individuals. It gives a clear structure to help people make investment choices and realize their progress. Working one step at a time toward every milestone, investors can consistently create income from dividends that support their financial security down the road.

Avoiding Analysis Paralysis

Having simplicity and efficiency is very important for anyone who follows a busy routine when it comes to dividend investing. Forming a smooth routine allows investors to keep track of their investments with very little time, avoiding the negative effects of over-analysis. A short and effective monitoring procedure can speed up decision-making, so you only need around 30 minutes a month to handle your portfolio.

This method relies on checking each month what matters most in terms of the health of the investment portfolio. It consists of looking at all the dividend payments, any alerts you get, and your overall holding of various stocks. In this way, investors are able to determine if they should review or make alterations in their investments. It allows the company to know when to wait and when it should change its strategy.

A way to deal with too much information is to follow only a few news sources and set a time to go through the updates all at once. It is helpful to set a calendar reminder to make sure you regularly check your portfolio on a quarterly basis. Following this approach makes it easier to remove unimportant signals and pay attention to critical alerts, which saves you from overreacting to any minor changes in the market.

For a lot of people, analysis paralysis happens when they become confused and fail to act because there is too much to look through. In this situation, having a guide for resolving these symptoms is very useful. Instead of rushing to act on every market shift, investors should consider using a '24-hour rule', which tells them to reconsider any sell or buy decision the day after.

Besides, learning to avoid watching your portfolio many times daily can encourage you to use a sensible approach. By determining the frequency of reviewing investments, people can focus better and avoid stress while managing their routines.

Anyone who has a hard time deciding what to do should set standards for the events that would require action. This step requires picking out certain events that lead to changes in the portfolio, for example, a big change in the company's dividend or its financial reports. If you already know what the triggers are, you can handle decisions faster and experience less worry about always looking at the market.

Essentially, preventing analysis paralysis involves finding good information and keeping things simple at the same time. Following a simple but secure routine, investors make sure their investments help them reach their goals despite the many statistics in the market. Using this method, investors put less effort into saving time and enjoying their experience more, which helps them earn steady growth from dividends in the long run.

Chapter 09: Leveraging Community and Resources

Engaging with Investment Communities

Being a part of investment communities can greatly influence investors of any level in the field of dividend investing. Such communities exist on forums, groups on social media, and investment platforms, and they are places where people exchange knowledge and provide support. Involvement in these networks lets investors grow faster, witness current trends, and gather advice on their choosing of stocks.

The worth of being involved in such groups is due to the many different perspectives and stories that its members share. You can join lively groups on Bogle heads and r/dividends, as well as read the comments on Seeking Alpha to exchange advice and debate which dividend stocks are good. Such interactions offer a lot of knowledge that helps investors improve their actions and stay away from typical errors.

Getting involved with the proper communities is very important. You should only follow reputable forums that do not let commercials influence their discussions. People should choose to invest in different communities rather than in those led by affiliate marketers or those known for "pump and dump" to prevent themselves from making bad financial choices. Thus, people should select organizations that put importance on knowledge, assistance, and following ethical guidelines when investing.

Taking part in these communities means you must be active. Revealing your achievements, bringing up important points, and marking successes together are top ways to interact positively. People gain new knowledge for themselves and share it with everyone else. Having regular talks with others and joining in group activities on the platform may provide steady support and encouragement.

Besides, these communities tend to share useful information that can guide investors. Notifications about certain stocks or types of investing make sure people are aware of what is happening. Going to ongoing educational sessions and chat events run by these communities can support your progress and help you meet new professionals.

The benefits of participation in investment communities go further than just getting advice. By doing so, they offer support and make sure people are responsible, especially because investing usually happens alone. Having the support of peers can inspire investors to keep moving toward their long-term aims, even if the market Is not favorable.

Being involved in investment groups can greatly boost an investor's performance and satisfaction in dividend investing. Such communities give people opportunities to learn and, at the same time, foster a feeling of unity among investors. Being a member of suitable forums and actively participating enables investors to get resources and advice that help them tackle the difficulties found in the financial markets.

Finding Reliable Resources

If you are in the world of dividend investing, looking for reliable resources is similar to journeying through an ocean with a map for financial success. You must be careful and use a plan since finding reliable data is very important. Although investing is full of information, it takes a skill to choose useful data from useless data.

You should first find out all the resources you have access to. People who invest should become familiar with the different kinds of sources available. Historically, people use company financial statements, annual reports, and official press releases when looking at primary sources. Using these papers, one can see the company's present financial status, its dividend policies, and predictions for the future. Some examples of secondary sources are financial news websites, investment blogs, and analyst reports, which give detailed explanations of market developments and the opinions of experts.

Credibility is something that must always be considered when you choose your resources. Trusted companies such as Bloomberg and The Wall Street Journal publish news based on strict journalism guidelines. Similarly, platforms like Morningstar and Seeking Alpha are valued for providing plenty of data and informative analysis. Platforms like these usually offer both spontaneous content by people and sound advice from professionals.

Because of the digital age, people can count on online forums and communities. On such websites as the r/dividends subreddit and the Bogle heads forum, you can benefit from the advice and encouragement of others. Even so, you should judge the information you find on forums since advice can be different for all kinds of investors.

These tools help to narrow down a huge number of possible dividend stocks. Finviz and Yahoo Finance give users a chance to set certain standards to limit their selections by yield, payout ratio, and past dividend growth history. On these sites, investors can set up their searches depending on what is most important for their investment goals.

In addition, you can learn a lot from newsletters and podcasts that offer information on dividend investing. You can use The Dividend Guy Blog or Dividend Growth Investor to stay updated about changes in the market, interesting chances, and trends related to dividends. Most of these resources simplify finances so that you can understand them and put the tips to use.

Although online tools and resources are very useful, teachers should also focus on traditional ways of teaching. Talking with other investors and joining financial events can give you valuable knowledge and bring you in contact with people who think in the same way as you. Getting advice from experts who work in financial services can give you advice that is suited to your needs and goals.

Being alert is very important when you're looking for reliable resources. People who invest should watch out for bias and interests that may guide stock or strategy recommendations without proper facts. Referring to more than one source helps to identify accurate facts and get a better understanding of the topic.

In the end, reliable resources for dividend investing come from gathering a set of trustworthy news sources that you improve over time. Using reliable resources from different sources, investors can guide their investments in dividend stocks with confidence and make their portfolios grow steadily.

Sharing and Learning from Peers

Being part of a financial community helps you learn a lot and advance in dividend investing. In forums, groups, and peer communities, these groups prove very useful to investors with any level of experience. People who become members of such groups learn faster, get new ideas, and keep up-to-date on the latest advice for dividend investing.

The main advantage of joining such a community is that you get to benefit from other members' experiences. Most members share what they have learned from their achievements and disappointments, giving others a lot of useful information. To give an example, Bogle heads, dividends on Reddit, and the comments section of Seeking Alpha have folks who are known for their active participation and knowledge. Such platforms let investors ask their questions, update each other with achievements, and get useful assistance, allowing everyone to learn more together.

You should always check that the communities you select are highly respected and not full of exaggerations. Communities that are widely trusted concentrate on education and help instead of sales and marketing. Investors need to choose groups that are against "pump and dump" and do not use a lot of affiliate marketing. With the help of a good community, members are more likely to choose well, as it emphasizes honest talks and useful advice, not aggressive approaches.

The place is welcoming to people who actively take part in these discussions. Receiving feedback from peers becomes easier if you talk about how your research is going and discuss important stages. Being involved in investing is beneficial for each individual as well as the general community since it promotes education and growth. Using community resources also lets people receive education and stay motivated. You can turn on alerts to learn when someone starts a new thread or chooses to participate in regular online gatherings.

For people who are motivated by achievements, joining monthly ones or taking part in crafting a strategic portfolio can be very fulfilling. In addition to promoting good investing, they also let individuals share their knowledge and methods with others. When investors are part of a community and share the same goals, they tend to remain determined to meet their long-term goals.

The main benefit of the community in dividend investing is that you can use the help and knowledge shared by discussing it with others. By learning from experienced investors, shareholders can improve their knowledge, improve the methods they apply, and enjoy alliances that will help them succeed financially. With the help of forums on the Internet or meetings nearby, you can meet other investors and exchange both encouragement and useful advice about your investments.

Staying Updated and Educated

Since dividend investing is constantly changing, it is important to keep learning and to stay informed. The financial markets keep changing with the arrival of new changes, new laws, and fresh trends.

If investors want to handle these changes, they should focus on learning and making changes as things progress.

Using financial news platforms and analysis tools is an important method to be kept informed. Seeking Alpha and Yahoo! are two trouble-free sources to use. They give users details about the market as well as a detailed analysis of dividend stocks. With these platforms, individuals can get custom alerts about key dates, including ex-dividend, newly announced payouts, and company earnings, so they are always up-to-date about events that matter to their portfolio.

Besides the main tools, getting newsletters and listening to podcasts about finance can provide more details and the views of experts on market movements and how to use dividends. The Dividend Guy Blog and Sure Dividend regularly post analyses and updates that are meant for people who focus on dividends. These resources may contain actual case reviews and interviews with professionals, which can provide extra ideas and approaches.

Another way to learn more is by joining and reading investor groups. Members of Bogle heads and r/dividends share and exchange useful ideas about investing on forums. In these groups, people discuss strategies, talk about what they have experienced, and inspire each other. You should try to locate communities that want to learn instead of those that revolve around making money or excitement.

Making a regular plan for monitoring and studying may help keep you from getting overwhelmed by information. For example, plan some events in your schedule for reviewing your portfolio and checking the latest news, as it can help you avoid information overload. With the help of tools, it is possible to concentrate on the most engaging and important news.

Education helps people know more about finances, respond to changes in their situation, and update their strategies. If you deal with retirement, get an inheritance, or have a major money issue, you need to rethink your investment plans. Being able to adapt plays a big role in staying dependable with your investments.

In addition, Apps and automated notices can help an investor watch their money with ease. Such tools offer information on dividend increase, yield, and portfolio return so that investors can decide what to do with their investments using facts.

All in all, dividend investing requires being armed with adequate tools, engaging with other investors, and staying updated with all kinds of changes. When you approach finances actively, it is easier to decide which investments to make, and it also ensures you reach your financial targets in the future.

Chapter 10: Real-World Case Studies

Successful Long-Term Investors

The practice of dividend investing is usually praised for helping people obtain financial security and build wealth in the long term. Successful long-term investors tend to stick to their rules, be patient, and know how compounding can help them. They realize that devoting energy to buying and selling shares is not as effective as consistently picking stocks that provide regular dividends and can deal with changes in the market.

Having a long-term outlook is one of the major factors that make an investor successful in the long run. Catalogers realize that the stock market can be unpredictable, and short-term changes usually happen. Rather than changing their approach with every market news, these people look at the long run since dividends are a steady income source regardless of the market's state. Putting the income back into investments leads to a growing amount when interest is earned. When an investment earns returns, those returns are then used to generate additional income, and this is a basic way that investors expand their wealth more and more as years go by.

Besides, they are able to spot companies that have solid fundamentals. They try to discover companies with a history of dividends and strong enough finances to sustain and possibly raise dividends in the future. It is necessary to review the company's financial statements, cash flow, and rate of earnings growth for analysis. Most successful investors choose companies that do well compared to others, have competent leaders, and can maintain revenues and dividends even in tough times.

Diversification is another key trait of these investors. They realize that spreading money into different sectors helps them deal with risks. Consequently, they avoid big losses if companies in any sector do poorly or the economy changes in a bad way. When creating a dividend portfolio, it helps to have both stocks giving quick income and stocks offering longer-term benefits.

Moreover, staying calm and focused is an important quality for any prolonged investor. Because they remain focused on their plans, these investors avoid major mistakes caused by market fluctuations. It is important to ensure that people do not act abruptly and endanger their hard work in investing. Setting up set rules for buying and selling allows them to keep their course through any rough times in the market.

In addition, they always work on improving their understanding and adjusting to new market trends. They pay attention to global investments, the tax situations involved, and what technological changes may affect them. By carrying out these steps, they guarantee that their strategies stay up to date. Due to their readiness to adapt and keep learning, skilled long-term investors can carefully select stocks and retain their wealth.

Learning from Mistakes

Learning from one's experiences in dividend investing can have a major effect on how successful the strategy becomes over the years. Building experience from investing often means you juggle many trials and face errors, as doing so teaches you a lot along the way. If you notice the value these lessons have, you can use your 'mistakes' to strengthen your investment strategy.

People going into dividend investments usually have high hopes based on the idea that dividends will provide steady income and increase their assets. Still, it is a fact that even experienced investors face difficulties. The most important thing is to accept mistakes as chances to learn. All of these errors teach us new lessons about how the market works and the details behind dividend payments.

Since dividend stocks are promising, some buyers listen to the high yields and overlook whether these dividends are sustainable. Wishing to get large rewards fast can be tempting, but often, such investments involve more risks. Sometimes, companies that promise big dividends are doing so since their stock has decreased due to other challenges. Sometimes, this leads the investor to experience a dividend trap and end up with stock value that has decreased because the payout was reduced. It is important to notice signs such as high dividend payout, declining earnings, and taking on more debt, as these may indicate a problem. With a deeper analysis of these indicators, investors can steer clear of problems and make smarter decisions.

Often, investors find out the hard way how necessary it is to be diversified. Investing everything in high-yield sectors can bring extra risks since such sectors are more likely to be affected by tough economies. If the market slows down, companies could reduce their dividend payments, which harms the income of many investors. By adding investments across different industries and the world, you can lower the risk to your portfolio.

Mistakes in the market can happen if traders are not careful of price changes. Feelings in the market can encourage investors to sell off in a hurry or to put all their money into 'hot' stocks, making it hard to reach their financial goals over the years. Sticking to set guidelines for purchase and sale helps investors continue through tough financial situations. Rather than being impressed by temporary changes in price, this field counts on knowing how dividend-paying stocks work.

In addition, lifelong learning and willingness to adapt are extremely important. Uniform strategies do not necessarily remain effective every day since conditions in markets change all the time. Monitoring updates in the markets, laws, and indicators of the economy allows investors to change their strategies for success. To keep up and improve, you can network with investment partners, register for seminars, and read books about money and Finance.

It is also important for every dividend investor to remain patient and have a long-term attitude. Reinvesting your dividends can lead to great wealth, but you have to wait for some time to see the full result. Aspiring for fast results might prompt a person to make decisions that interrupt the healthy development of their portfolio.

In all, mistakes play a big role in the learning process of dividend investors. If investors take what happened in the past seriously, they build a stronger and more effective way to invest and reach their finances.

Turnaround Success Stories

When we look at dividend investing, examples of companies that made a comeback prove how determined and smart these businesses are. They are also concerned with the actions and discipline used to restore a company's success after facing difficulties. People who have gotten through tough situations with strength can show us how vital patience, focus, and knowing how to change is.

Let's review what an investor experienced when the market went through a major crash. Taking control of the situation, this person opted for a careful review and carried out decisions with discipline. First, they studied each stock in their portfolio, singling out good candidates who were currently low in value but had a strong past and bright prospects. This investor chose to focus on companies that had enough assets, manageable liabilities, and a regular record of paying dividends at all times.

The investor did not only react but took the initiative by affecting the market. Items and funds in technology and healthcare allowed the investor to reap positive rewards after the market rebound. To use this strategy, one needed to focus on industry trends and be aware of the economic reasons affecting recovery. Besides, the investor invested in a wide variety of assets in various regions, so any losses in one sector would be offset by other sectors.

What sticks out in this case is an investor who noticed that a company reduced its dividend on a main stock. Since this was considered an opportunity, the investor used it to review his portfolio thoroughly. They checked if the dividend cut was caused by difficulties that would shift or those that might prove to be long-lasting. After the analysis, I could decide whether to keep, sell, or replace stocks by properly assessing what each company was capable of in the future.

This time, a dividend investor had to deal with shifts and fluctuations in the market. Using discipline in DRIPs meant the investor decided to buy more shares whenever stock prices decreased and was able to receive more income in dividends later on, saving money. By reinvesting during the downs, this approach indicated how following a strict method can help make weaknesses in the market beneficial.

Such stories prove that having self-control and looking ahead is necessary for successful dividend investing. People who succeed in turnarounds usually keep their cool when faced with challenges, adjust their strategies, and are fully informed about the businesses they invest in. They also believe that constantly learning and being aware of changes in the market matter a lot.

However, companies that succeed in turning around demonstrate the major effect of maintaining a strong strategy. While it is clear that downturns in the market exist, they create new chances for anyone ready and open to change. By emphasizing the basics, keeping their investments spread, and being patient, investors are able to get through challenges and make progress in the future.

Extracting Actionable Lessons

Those involved in dividend investing discover most of their lessons by practicing on real investments. Having the capability to turn such experiences into helpful actions lets investors improve their plans.

Learning from other people's successes and failures can guide you to better decisions.

Looking into detailed case studies is one of the best ways to get useful lessons from the actions of others. Besides pointing out how things are done well, these narratives also indicate the usual mistakes that can be avoided. Considering the experience of a long-term investor who keeps reinvesting dividends displays how discipline plays a key role in building a big portfolio. These examples prove that reinvesting dividends helps wealth grow gradually, so even small and consistent savings can result in a lot of money.

At the same time, warning cases of dividend traps teach us about the importance of managing risks. In these cases, some high-yield stocks may appear strong at first sight, but they actually have major financial problems. Investors who lost dividends due to weak financial policies or difficulties in their sector understand why it's important to do a good assessment before investing. With the help of such narratives, investors know to be wary of companies that give out large payouts or have earnings falling.

Also, examples of turnarounds where investors showed strength in dealing with market changes teach others what resilience is about. It is common for investors to stick to a diversified portfolio and keep following a defined strategy. Many times, these stories suggest that looking forward and hesitating to act on each market change can result in overcoming losses and becoming successful. The focus on spreading investments across different industries and countries is helpful because it lessens risks and keeps earnings stable when things are rough.

Taking all this into account, there are several habits that anyone interested in dividends can follow. Reviewing your portfolio on a regular basis is the main thing that matters. Doing this requires checking the performances of assets, reexamining the proportion in each sector, and increasing or reducing a portion where the market shifts. If a portfolio is regularly monitored and balanced, it stays in line with what an investor wants and can handle in terms of risk.

A strong way to look for potential dividend stocks is by putting in place a strong screening process. You should lay out what you look for in the results, the rate of returns, and the company's history of increasing dividends. Investors ' strategic objectives can be aligned with impressive dividend stocks by making use of financial screeners and analyst reports.

Understanding how to manage emotions plays an important role in real-life investing. The tendency to keep calm and not sell when the markets fall is usually what sets successful investors apart from others. Considering the dividends and a patient approach can ease investors' concerns during short-term ups and downs in the market.

In general, successful dividend investing relies greatly on the ability to learn from the experience of others. Learning from other people's experiences helps individuals craft a way of investing that leads to more stable growth from dividends.

Chapter 11: Automation and Consistency

Setting Up DRIPs

With a Dividend Reinvestment Plan (DRIP), investors follow some important strategies that secure the automatic reinvestment of dividends and may lead to higher returns. This strategy is good for people who want their dividends to buy more shares, resulting in more dividends and greater growth.

Choosing the proper broker is an important start when you begin DRIP. A number of main firms across the US, UK, Canada, and Australia let investors use DRIP services, yet the features aren't always the same. People who plan to use DRIPs should start by checking which platforms they can use and the conditions that come with the plans. Some brokers may be able to provide DRIPs for a limited number of stocks and put rules on buying fractional shares. You need to grasp these important points to avoid facing complications in the future.

After selecting a brokerage, you should look into the account settings to turn on the DRIP option. Relatively, it works with a few simple clicks on the platform, though sometimes it needs to be set up manually. An investor could find that methods for setting up a DRIP in Fidelity in the US are compared to what's done in Hargreaves Lansdown in the UK. In order to set up the platform correctly, investors should check the broker's guide in the support area.

DRIPs are advantageous because they can automatically reinvest your dividends for people who prefer not to handle investing regularly. Because dividends are automatically reinvested, investors of DRIPs can keep their approach to investing regular and dependable. Still, before choosing automatic reinvestment, it is wise to consider both positives and negatives, such as when an investor wants the dividends to provide income or when the market is causing uncertainties.

Be sure to think about the tax effects that come with joining a DRIP. In various areas, the government still treats dividends in the form of reinvestment as a source of taxable income. You should keep records well to make sure taxes are filed correctly, and the cost basis of the new stock reflects the changes. Investors need to learn about their country's tax rules and consider getting help from a tax expert to handle these matters well.

If someone meets difficulties with stocks or shares, having some troubleshooting tips on hand can be very useful. Those who have difficulty can either contact their broker's service or opt for other methods, for instance, reinvesting shares through their account or choosing stocks that suit DRIPs. If some stocks are missing from the broker's DRIP plan, choosing an alternative provider might be better.

All things considered, organizing DRIP calls for considering automation as well as staying alert to your strategy. If investors understand how DRIPs work and make them match their financial goals, they can increase the growth potential of their investments again and again.

Automating Contributions

Automatic investments in your accounts make it easier to build a strong dividend investing approach by avoiding the emotional influences that make decision-making more challenging. Automating the system enables investors to stick to their objectives with less effort.

The initial part of automating is to plan a schedule for your giving that fits in with your finances. It is possible if you establish scheduled moves of funds from your checking account into your investment account. There are various ways to manage your transfers with the help of some brokerage platforms and banks. You may choose to have $100 transferred from your bank to your brokerage account every month. This consistent approach not only makes your investment process simple but also less risky, thanks to the dollar-cost averaging strategy.

It is very important to modify these contributions whenever your finances shift. When your income, spending, or aims in finances change, look into making changes to the amount you contribute. Although keeping your strategy in place is useful, make sure to revisit it now and then to check that it fits your financial situation. When your income goes up, this may include increasing your savings. On the other hand, you could cut back a bit when you are under financial stress.

Automated investments enable you to overcome mental obstacles that might stop you from investing regularly. Several investors find it hard not to buy or sell based on market trends or avoid putting money in when the market drops. Using automatic contributions, you avoid these mood-based problems, so your investments keep following the same plan no matter what the market does. Using this strategy, people prefer to accumulate money over time, ignoring short-term ups and downs in the market.

In addition, by setting up automation, you can invest without noticing the direct effect on your finances. If you use methods like transferring some of your pay to your investment account, a part of your income will go straight to your goals, so you won't need to worry about it each month.

Sticking with regular and automatic investments can strongly affect your financial situation. You can see on a growth chart how regular contributions can earn a lot over the years, thanks to simple compounding. By viewing the visuals, people are encouraged to stick with a well-planned investment approach.

Also, dealing with mental challenges is important for successful automated investing. Setting up an automatic routine makes it simpler for investors to work on their portfolios without having to follow them closely. Sticking to the system allows people to support their finances now and also set their minds on growing their wealth over time, which strengthens their overall financial stability.

Using Custom Templates

Using personalized and adjustable resources in dividend investing can greatly boost the process of following and organizing one's portfolio. Custom templates allow investors to adapt their tracking systems according to what they need and want. These tools change with an investor's progress, giving detailed information and helping to understand how your finances are growing.

The first part of using custom templates is realizing that they help turn data into something you can use. When both monthly and annual dividend income are tracked in templates, investors can see their cash flow, notice important patterns, and decide which actions to take next. Thus, these templates help to organize new investments, increase dividends, and keep track of reinvestments so that all relevant information about the portfolio stays updated.

The main advantage of good custom templates is that they can supervise essential metrics such as yield, rate of growth, and achievement of dividend goals. With automatic calculation, investors do not have to waste time and can avoid possible mistakes. This way of handling data helps improve results while giving investors time to think about making the right decisions.

Besides, custom spreadsheets can add color-coded alerts that let the user know when a company makes changes in their dividends or income. They help investors realize their concerns and urge them to explore the situation and take the required actions. With these alerts, investors can easily anticipate and handle possible problems.

As well as watching your money and its growth, templates help encourage you to mark your achievements. Having particular, measurable goals, for example, receiving annual dividend income that covers your monthly bills or higher, gives you a feeling of progress and benefits your positive investing pattern. If charts or graphs are used to track these key steps, it becomes clear to see how the investment is developing, and staying committed to the approach is easier.

Having ready-made templates lets you make decisions when investing by reducing decision-making stress. A simple but powerful monitoring system allows investors to see their portfolio's well-being clearly and without getting confused. Doing a quick dashboard check each month keeps investors informed and also protects them from excessive and stressful monitoring.

To sum up, using these templates is wise because they are useful both in logistics and in the investor's mindset. A customized system for tracking and monitoring investments helps people make better decisions, see their development as time goes on, and manage their investments properly. As a result of this method, achieving financial goals becomes much clearer, which boosts investors' abilities to deal with market challenges confidently.

Maintaining Discipline

Being disciplined when investing in dividends is crucial for anyone who wants financial security in the future. Emotional well-being and smart ways of investing are just a few of the many features of this discipline. Emotion can be the toughest opponent an investor deal with. During uncertain periods in the market, people may do things that interfere with the strategy they had planned. Investors should learn to stop, look at their information, and review their investment strategy whenever they want to make a quick decision. When you use the 24-hour rule, it could calm you down and give you enough time to weigh your actions before selling too quickly.

Additionally, automation helps a lot in keeping discipline. If investors use DRIPs and plan regular purchases, the effect of emotions on their decisions will be reduced, so their strategy stays consistent and objective. With automation, investors are able to pursue their long-term plans without getting distracted by fluctuations in the market.

It is also very important to diversify your investments following this method. To reduce risks and have a regular income during hard times, investors should put their money in different sectors and countries. With this approach, companies withstand conflicts in their sectors and also remain safe amid widespread economic downturns. A diversified portfolio helps the investor stay calm during unexpected changes in the market.

Besides, it's wise to keep some money that you can put to good use when the right investment opportunity emerges. You should save some money so that new opportunities or surprise costs won't twist your main investment plan. In this way, investors do not need to unload their holdings when liquidity is short.

An investor's discipline can be strengthened by remembering past events. A review of past market downturns and of how dividend portfolios did can reassure investors in their approach. As a result of the 2008–2009 Global Financial Crisis, dividend-focused portfolios managed to give stable income to investors even when the stock market suffered. Awareness of history can give investors strength to continue sticking to their strategy.

It is necessary to review your portfolio on a regular basis. While analyzing these investments, it is important to observe how they would fare during recessions, controlling those payout ratios, amounts of debt, and their previous dividend records. By taking this approach, companies can fix possible problems before they turn into major dangers.

Disciplined dividend investing means you need to regulate your emotions, plan your portfolio, keep it diverse, learn from experience, and check it often. When these concepts are used, investors are able to find their way through the market inconveniences with composure and reach their financial dreams.

Chapter 12: Adapting to Life Changes

Adjusting for Retirement

It can be hard for many investors to change from saving their money to spending it. When you come close to retirement, your investments are better suited for making money and keeping it secure. People should rebalance their investments to fit new financial conditions and levels of risk they are comfortable with.

One of the main things to do when preparing for retirement is to move your assets to more suitable places. You should slowly change from high-growth investments to ones that give more consistent income. So, investors might add more shares of companies that give out dividends or invest more in bonds and high-yield REITs. The objective is to have an investment portfolio that generates regular income to take over the money workers get from their jobs.

It is also crucial to decide on how to withdraw funds from the market. Retirees should have a proper plan for using the money from their investments. One must generally determine the safe withdrawal rate to ensure that your funds will be enough to last. It is common to follow the 4% rule, which allows people to withdraw 4% of their portfolio's total annually after considering inflation. In fact, this rule can be changed to match the retiree's health, spending habits, and any other money coming in.

Managing risks is much more important in retirement than at other times. Investors should be ready for the ups and downs in the market and any economic slowdowns, which may lower their retirement savings. It is important to spread your investments to avoid risks. If retirees have investments in a range of asset classes and sectors, the bad results of one investment won't greatly hurt their portfolio.

Regularly checking your portfolio is necessary when your circumstances or the financial market changes. Anyone who has retired should assess their approach to investing from time to time to maintain fit with their circumstances and risks. It may call for rearranging the investment mix to meet the desired asset portion or changing the plan for withdrawing funds due to major market upheavals.

Making good use of tax laws is very important when planning for retirement. People who retire need to realize how their various sources of income are taxed and use special accounts to keep their taxes low. If you put stocks that pay dividends into a tax-favored account, the taxes you have to pay are lower, and the remaining funds can be used more easily.

Seeking advice from a financial expert could be very important before or after retirement. Retirees who meet with a financial advisor can learn a lot about today's financial decisions and how to handle complex aspects of their finances. An advisor can help by offering strategies that are fit for a particular retiree's financial and personal needs.

Overall, when someone is about to retire, they should carefully revise and reorganize their financial strategy. While making an investment plan, people should keep their income demands, risk strategies, tax factors, and portfolio maintenance in mind. Adopting proactive measures can give retirees sufficient support for their needs and a pleasant retirement.

Handling Windfalls

Getting a large sum of money suddenly, be it by inheritance, a bonus, or another way, usually feels both thrilling and challenging. The main thing to remember when facing a sudden windfall is to use strategy and think through every choice. The first thing to do is to fight the desire to act rashly because of FOMO or get rich suddenly. It's much better to use a step-by-step process that helps you reach your long-term money targets.

Check how your finances are at the moment and spot which of your current needs the windfall could cover. For example, you may choose to get rid of high-interest debt, build up an emergency fund, or look after needed repairs in your house. Making these areas your main focus means the windfall will support your future.

Following the urgent situations, think about the benefits of phased investing. The process calls for buying different investments over time instead of spending all the money at the beginning. Using a phased process can handle risks created by market ups and downs. If you get $50,000 unexpectedly, you may select to place some in a mixture of stocks and bonds and leave the remaining cash or other short-term assets. When market conditions change over the following months, you are free to add more money to your portfolio as dips and chances arise.

You should adjust your strategy if something unforeseen, such as a new situation in life or a reduction in income, happens. Unexpected things like losing employment, high medical bills, or changes in your family situation can cause you to check your financial plan. If unexpected costs appear, you may want to stop reinvesting your dividends, drop your savings rate, or change your portfolio to fit the updated budget.

You should check your financial plan from time to time and when something important in your life occurs. In this way, your investments continue to fit your objectives and the amount of risk you are ready to take. Having periodic re-evaluations of your financial position is useful, and you could do this annually or every other year.

Being involved with people who have similar investment interests can help you, too. These groups and networks give you tips, keep you up to date, and motivate you to learn about opportunities in the market. Such communities may give you useful advice and make you accountable for sharing your achievements, asking for help, and acknowledging your achievements.

Going from having a windfall to possessing lasting wealth is the main aim in handling such sudden income. If you manage the windfall by focusing long term, being open to different ideas, and using a positive mindset, you can make good use of this unplanned wealth.

Dealing with Setbacks

Many times, investing in dividends brings up problems that can trip up even the world's best fund manager. No matter the reason for such delays, it is important to keep your long-term financial ambitions from changing course.

Job loss is a typical issue that investors have to overcome. When your salary goes down suddenly, it becomes tougher to put money into investment accounts. During these circumstances, people should consider their financial goals and make appropriate corrections. It may be necessary to stop or lower the amount you invest in dividends. Flexibility is important so that investors can change their approach when necessary, due to financial changes.

The strategy can be interrupted if you end up facing unexpected expenses. Unexpected fees for health or house repairs tend to take away money that could be invested. Doing this, having a cash reserve is a sensible move. The reserve gives the company financial backing, so it doesn't have to sell investments quickly whenever unplanned expenses arise.

Adding a new baby to the family or a major event can stop investors from sticking to their plans. Such changes usually mean people have to reconsider their financial targets and risk levels. When they have a new family member, many individuals decide to stop aiming for big returns and focus instead on making steady money. It is important to check your investment plan regularly, mainly when big life events occur, to see if it fits your new financial situation.

In addition, when the overall economy weakens, it poses a big challenge for dividend investors. When there are recessions or market corrections, it may be very tempting to act on impulse. On the other hand, it's important to stick to good habits. Combining investment in various industries and ensuring a mix of safe, high-yield, and fast-growing stocks may reduce the effect of market fluctuations. It is also wise to have parts of your investments in sectors like consumer staples or utilities, which tend to keep performing better when the economy slows down.

It is clear from all of this that having emotional strength is key. Dealing with the stress that comes with investing issues often depends on how people's emotions are controlled. If people fall victim to emotions, such as panic selling or trying to gain more profits, they may end up with decisions that harm their finances. It is, therefore, very important to aim for long-term progress instead of being influenced by day-to-day market changes. Putting your investments on autopilot and sticking to the plan lowers emotional risk and keeps your investment plan on the right course.

All in all, obstacles are something you should expect when investing. Nonetheless, using flexible tactics, making sure there is enough cash at hand, and being disciplined with feelings enable investors to cope well with such issues. Keep going over your investment plan and keep changing it as things change to avoid losing focus on your long-term plans. To invest successfully in dividends means to create wealth as well as to preserve it from the impacts of life's challenges.

Reviewing Plans Regularly

Regulating your investment strategies is very important for making your portfolio strong and progressive in dividend investing. In this practice, people regularly look at their financial strategies and modify them as required by new market trends and their own goals. When they reflect on their investments, people can make certain their portfolio will hold up no matter what changes the market brings.

Understanding that routine checks are different from action triggers is the main thing you need to know. Routine monitoring is important to keep everything in the portfolio moving as planned, and action triggers occur when certain market developments or personal events call for a change in how investments are made. Those who invest in the stock market should learn to spot these changes; for example, when a company adjusts its dividend program, changes in the economy occur, or somebody experiences retirement or a different amount of income.

Investors should use careful plans to prevent becoming confused by the information they receive. If you cut down the number of news sources, collect the updates at once, and organize regular times to review, it becomes simpler to pay attention. For example, an investment portfolio reviews every three months enables investors to check results and fix anything that needs addressing without always having to watch it closely.

A big aspect of frequent reviewing is being able to avoid analysis paralysis. When too much information is given to investors, it can stop them from deciding what to do. This can be solved by providing a troubleshooting guide that deals with typical signs of analysis paralysis. It may also suggest the "24-hour rule" that delays buy or sell actions for a whole day unless regular rebalancing is needed.

In addition, creating specific and clear ways to review your portfolio matters a lot. To do this, you might need a list to review your dividends, examine any alerts you receive, and check how your money is spread among different investments. With a list in hand, investors can go through every part of their portfolio and not miss anything.

Apart from reviewing their investments, investors need to manage possible risks and respond when the market drops suddenly. You should also grasp the consequences of reduced dividends and decide how to restore the income through rebalancing the portfolio. DRIPs and making fresh investments are useful approaches for reaching better results and overcoming investor worries in tough times.

Finally, using a disciplined and simple system goes with your long-term plans and prevents you from falling for over-trading and other risks. Regularly reviewing their investments and sticking to a good plan, investors find it much easier to deal with the difficulties of dividend investing. Taking time to review the portfolio often keeps it safe from risks and helps it grow steadily in the future.

Chapter 13: Exploring Advanced Strategies

Dividend ETFs and REITs

For people who invest in dividends, Dividend Exchange-Traded Funds (ETFs) and Real Estate Investment Trusts (REITs) have a strong reputation for diversifying your portfolio and upping your returns. Since they are structured differently and depend on various assets, both instruments help create a dependable dividend portfolio.

A Dividend ETF collects dividend-paying stocks, so investors get immediate exposure to companies in various fields and countries. Since diversification covers many stocks, people who like convenience choose this approach because they don't need to do much research on each one. With dividend ETFs, people can take part in different dividend-paying companies in one place without acting on all individual stocks. It results in less money spent on transactions and helps lower the risks from individual stock prices. An example is the Vanguard Dividend Appreciation ETF (VIG), which makes it simple to obtain a list of companies that have a record of increasing their dividends.

If you want to invest in real estate ownership, the easy way is through REITs. Because they are required to distribute most of their taxable income as dividends, they interest investors who look for higher returns. Because REITs cover different industries, they make it possible for investors to access real estate markets that are not available to them directly. There are several special risks involved with REITs; for example, their value can rise or fall a lot depending on interest rates and the condition of the property sector. Investing in the broad meaning, a US REIT ETF like VNQ enables you to get a diversified real estate portfolio, with the chance to make high-yield income and still manage risks properly.

Having international dividend stocks or ETFs in a portfolio gives extra diversification, lets you access international markets, and can lead to decent tax-related rewards. Investing globally comes with risks like currency movements and extra taxes, but it also connects you to countries that show changes in the economy and have their chances to grow. Focusing on the global market can be useful when your home country's market is going through great changes.

Usually, building a portfolio of dividends involves adding direct stock holdings, ETFs, and REITs so you benefit from their unique qualities. Among typical asset allocations in a model portfolio are 60% for US dividend stocks, 20% for ETFs, and 20% for REITs, which helps balance risk and chances for consistent growth. When using this strategy, investors get income from well-known US dividend stocks, the diverse benefits of ETFs, and the generous returns offered by REITs.

All in all, Dividend ETFs and REITs are vital tools for dividend investors since their different benefits complement each other and lead to a stronger and more profitable collection of investments. Proper control and usage of these instruments ensure that investors keep their income safe and can achieve steady growth in the future.

International Stocks

Holding international stocks opens a new possibility to add more types and more benefits to your dividend portfolio. Investing in foreign companies allows investors to diversify their sources of income and protect their money from the dangers linked to a single market. It gives investors access to promising markets with high profits and, at the same time, supports security by including developed markets that regularly pay dividends.

Since international stocks function under other regulations and economies, they can present some obstacles and offer some benefits compared to domestic stocks. It is very important to grasp these differences. For example, European firms may give out bigger dividends since people there prefer income gains, while developments in Asia create many growth possibilities. Investing in international stocks gives investors an opportunity to benefit from regional factors.

An advantage of having an international portfolio is the chance to invest in industries that are less developed at home. As an example, a U.S. investor could find that there are relatively few chances in luxury goods or global shipping, as these belong more to European and Asian economies. If you invest across borders, you can take part in these companies and enjoy the special strengths in their growth.

However, there are certain dangers and complications associated with buying international stock. Changes in currency values may have a large effect on returns. If the economy's currency values rise, it may negatively impact the profits, but when the currency is weak, it can help improve profits. That's why protecting the portfolio against currencies moving in the wrong direction using hedging methods is important.

How investment taxes work in another country is an important detail. Because every country's tax rules vary, the tax rates and treaties can have a direct impact on the dividend income that investors get. Knowing taxes on international dividends is useful, and one could use accounts that reduce taxes or invest in countries with beneficial tax treaties.

Besides, risks that affect countries can also cause concerns over international investments. If the country experiences political problems, altered regulations, or economic sanctions, it may influence the way a company operates and the way the market behaves overseas. Anyone picking international stocks should follow important announcements from governments and adjust their choices accordingly.

In spite of these issues, foreign stocks in a dividend portfolio might give you higher returns and some security from price swings in the domestic market. People who invest should look into ETFs that focus on international dividends as a way to spread their investment without complications. Holding these ETFs gives you exposure to many kinds of stocks from different nations, so there is less need to pick single shares.

All in all, investing in foreign stocks means focusing on income and also understanding the movements of global markets. Choosing suitable international equities offers investors a chance to be more diverse globally, earn better investment returns, and maintain their portfolio's strength during recessions at home. Therefore, including international stocks is very important for a solid dividend investing approach since they give investors both stability and growth opportunities for their portfolio.

Hybrid Income Strategies

When constructing hybrid income strategies for dividend investors, various asset classes serve as the core, helping the strategies make use of various benefits to create a reliable income stream. Besides diversification in stocks, you should approach it with a deliberate mix that has ETFs, REITs, and direct holdings. Every tool helps maintain the balance between risks, rewards, and the ease of converting assets to cash.

As a core element, this strategy uses dividend-focused ETFs to give easy and simple access to many companies that pay dividends. Traders use these ETFs to avoid selecting many stocks individually and get diversified immediately. Aggregating investments through a fund, ETFs help reduce the risks from companies' swings while gaining the majority of total market dividends. Since they charge less for management, they are a good choice for anyone who wants both growth and income from their investments.

Investments in REITs give hybrid income investors more diversification possibilities and income. Since REITs need to share a large part of their profits as dividends, they regularly offer higher returns than regular stocks. It makes sense in an environment with low interest rates since fixed-income investments may offer little profit. Investors need to consider that REITs are exposed to problems within the industry, for example, changes in real estate values and how sensitive they are to interest rates.

Adding individual dividend stocks to a hybrid income strategy allows people to choose those industries and companies that fit their financial objectives. Investing in stocks known for steady dividends and steady development may help you get sustained earnings and a chance for higher returns. The task includes thorough study and continued supervision to make sure dividends are secure, and the companies are in good condition.

To make a model hybrid portfolio, I would put 60% in ETFs, 20% in REITs, and 20% in individual dividend stocks. It tries to get the best results from earnings and investments by controlling risk. ETFs cover a wide range of income, REITs bring more money into your portfolio, and individual stocks help you grow in specified sectors.

You should manage your hybrid portfolio and keep your allocation consistent by regularly rebalancing it as the market changes. Investors need to decide how they will respond if the market or the investments' finances experience serious changes.

In the end, this approach to dividend investing is convenient and suits investors by enabling them to take advantage of different assets. When you carefully mix ETFs, REITs, and individual stocks, your portfolio can stand firm and give both steady income and chances for your funds to rise in various market situations.

Advanced Risk Management

It takes a detailed method of risk control to handle financial markets for those with dividend stocks effectively. Thus, investors must try to find ways to diversify their assets. Handling risks well in dividend investing requires using different approaches to save capital and give incomes a steady flow.

Being diversified is one of the most important things in advanced risk management. Despite the generally known term, real diversification means going beyond investing in a variety of stocks. To be successful, you should put resources in different sectors, regions, and types of investments. With this method, sector-related risks are lowered, and the portfolio is defended against downfalls that only impact some industries. As an illustration, in times of economic slowdowns, sections such as consumer staples and utilities are likely to do well, so investors seeking safety can consider these options.

Geographic diversification is just as important as being active in several stock sectors. When including international stocks or ETFs, investors lessen their impact from risks affecting one country's economy and politics. The plan both improves the portfolio's stability and presents chances to profit from emerging markets, where growth potential is usually greater than in developed ones.

A different high-quality strategy is selecting dividend-based exchange-traded funds and REITs, which focus on real estate investments. With these instruments, it is possible to gain quick access to sectors like real estate since these sectors are usually not well represented in a regular stock portfolio. Nevertheless, people investing in REITs should recognize that their performance can be greatly affected by both changing interest rates and problems in separate industries.

Having enough cash is also important for effective risk management. Having some money in cash or other near-cash assets gives investors an option to take advantage of new opportunities appearing during market troubles. When markets are unstable, and prices decrease, the "dry powder" way of investing becomes very helpful.

Checking a company's financial position is also an important thing to do. Taking a look at regular payout, debt, and profits can help investors confirm that the company can maintain dividends. If a company pays out too much of its income in dividends, it could struggle during hard economic periods and decide to reduce payouts.

Not only that but being disciplined emotionally plays a big role in managing risks properly. The fear that falls in the market causes investors to sell their assets, lowering the value of their portfolio. In such tough periods, investors are recommended to use certain rules and lists to support their actions and ensure their decisions depend on facts rather than feelings. Using Dividend Reinvestment Plans and having your investments scheduled can ensure you keep following an investment plan and earn more over the long run.

It is also necessary to keep learning and updating approaches in advanced risk management. Following the latest changes in markets, economic data, and taxes can allow investors to change their strategies in advance. Reaching out to investment communities and making use of tools and platforms designed for financial news can give you reliable information for making good choices.

The main idea of advanced risk management in dividend investing is to assemble a broad portfolio that stands firm against market volatility and eventually generates regular income. If investors use a strategy that entails diversification, managing cash, evaluating companies, and having emotional control, they will manage the markets in a safer and less stressful way.

Chapter 14: Conclusion and Next Steps

Reinforcing Core Lessons

It is extremely important to keep repeating the main principles of dividend investing. The main idea is to stick to the key rules that support successful investing, using them constantly to build financial security in the future. Going over these lessons again strengthens an investor's strategy and leads to higher accumulated wealth.

An important thing to learn about dividend investing is the strength of compounding. Following this principle, continuously reinvesting dividends can grow much more over the years. Investors can use dividends to buy new shares, which gives their returns for the future and more chances for dividend growth. When people repeat this process over the years, their little investments can become large wealth. To get the best returns, every investor must take advantage of the impacts of compounding.

Another main idea is that it is important to be diversified. Investing money in various sectors and different places helps reduce the risks caused by swings in the market. When a portfolio is diversified, one weak sector or area cannot cause major damage to the whole investment. This way of doing things prevents losses and supports entering new markets to help the company grow. Investors ought to examine and revise their portfolios on a regular basis to have a well-diversified investment approach.

Dealing with risks is very important for anyone practicing dividend investing. When investing, investors should keep an eye on how well the company is doing financially by considering its income, regular profits, and financial obligations. A proven track record of keeping and increasing dividends for a company shows that it is in good financial condition. Looking for companies that demonstrate stability and have regularly given dividends helps investors avoid the possibility of losing dividends.

Being patient and disciplined plays a big role in doing well with dividend investing. Since the market can change quickly, short-term ups and downs might be hard to handle. Still, if an investor keeps their eyes on the long-term plan and follows it, handling the market changes becomes less stressful. Since the approach is process-based, investors are pushed to stick to their long-term goals instead of being tempted by quick market changes.

It is important to keep learning and adapting if you want to maintain the key lessons in dividend investing. The financial sector keeps changing, and monitoring updates in the market, laws, and economy is very important. Joining financial communities, reading blog posts, and going through resources can teach investors new things and give them more informative strategies.

If they keep learning and acting on these basic points, investors are able to have a strong portfolio that faces challenges and takes advantage of growth opportunities. Adhering to these core beliefs allows investors to meet their financial targets and enjoy financial security.

Celebrating Milestones

Every milestone in dividend investing helps move you on your quest for financial security and development. Every achievement shows the investor's hard work, the right steps taken, and their patience. Some of these achievements are just the initial dividend income, and others mean your investment income is larger than your regular monthly living costs. Whenever a person invests, they show greater commitment and learn more about the world of investing.

Most of the time, reaching a dividend-related goal starts by establishing what you want to accomplish. The first target for their investing journey could be getting $100 in yearly dividends. The first target here is to learn how to invest in a focused and regular manner, not only to make a profit. When investors get paid dividends for the first time, they start to see that the money earned through investments can be used to motivate them further.

With time, the milestones an investor reaches also change to highlight greater accomplishments. Earnings from the stock market add up to the amount you pay for a household utility or phone bill, which motivates many people. Since dividends help cover daily costs, investors can truly benefit from them and use them to become financially independent.

Big and small achievements should be properly celebrated. Every momentous step forward should be recognized as a win. Celebrating, regardless of the form chosen, can praise one's progress and make people remain steadfast in their hard work. Such progress assures investors that they should stick with their investments, even when markets go through difficult times.

In addition, these moments offer chances for people to consider what has happened and make any needed changes. When they achieve their investment goals, people gain experience and realize which parts of their plans are effective and which parts should be improved. It is necessary to continually review and modify organization models to succeed for a long period. Thanks to this, investors can review their methods, arrange their investments better, and aim for something more challenging.

Having milestones gives investors something to concentrate on as they reach for their long-term aims. Whenever markets go up or down, these accomplishments influence investors to keep doing what they have been doing. They are there for stability and support since patience and persistence play a big role in archaeology.

The main purpose of marking dividend milestones is not limited to just celebrating these results. It is all about forming a lasting and fulfilling method of investing and having set objectives, praising what is achieved, and reviewing every stage to help investors strengthen their resilience. Using this mindset, investors support their goals and enjoy their investment experience from the start to the end.

Encouraging Continuous Learning

In dividend investing, you should never stop learning because that helps you adjust to changes in the market. Knowing all you can about the market allows you to make better choices and stick to strategies that are still effective in today's financial environment. Because the environment for dividend investing keeps changing, investors should always be astute and capable of reacting to new situations.

Learning is something investors should keep doing all the time. To do this, one must look for new details, interact with different opinions, and keep improving their understanding of financial matters. Accessing different educational resources, such as literature, online education, web conferences, and financial updates, lets you learn more about dividend stocks, future trends, and all elements of the economy.

Sectional meetings and taking part in the community help students keep learning. Going to investment forums, participating in seminars, and joining either clubs or online communities allows the sharing of ideas and experiences with many investors at once. People in these communities can work together to discuss methods, exchange information, and get suggestions for investing. Being involved in a similar community lets investors understand the latest market trends and encourages them with the support of others.

An important part of continuous learning is to use feedback and take time to consider the investment process. Analyzing past investing actions helps improve and boosts the overall strategy. In this process, people look at the results of their investments, recognize the reasons behind them, and look for ways to do better in the future. Looking back at their past achievements allows investors to improve their strategy and prevent duplicating the same errors.

Besides, technology has made it easier for people to get learning materials. Because of all the digital tools available today, users can easily find current data, see how markets are performing, and use thorough analysis techniques. By being able to use technology, investors can track recent developments, conduct thorough research, and make reliable decisions.

Being committed to learning means also knowing about bigger economic and financial factors that affect dividend investments. Apart from investment research, one should be aware of trends in the economy, interest rates, inflation levels, and important events around the globe. Knowledge of all these factors gives investors a chance to predict market changes and react accordingly.

All in all, you need to be a lifelong learner to do well in dividend investing. It enables investors to handle the difficulties found in the financial markets easily and quickly. Staying educated, teaming up with peers, assessing past actions, and relying on technology allow investors to do better in investments. Gaining knowledge about dividend investing boosts one's skills and improves the knowledge of the investment community.

Final Call to Action

At the key stage of dividend investing, the path that lies ahead gives people the chance to build financial security and stability. It is now easier for readers to use dividends to support a happy retirement because of the advice and approaches explained in this book. It should not just be seen as the finish of school but rather as a start to reaching financial dreams and turning them into realities.

The strength of dividend investing is that it changes the instability of markets into a regular income. If investors pick companies that earn and distribute stable dividends, their portfolios can remain strong in recessions as well. Taking this approach means being patient and having discipline, which shields investors from risks and troubles in the market.

Now is the time to use the knowledge learned. Make sure your financial goals and a dividend-oriented strategy match each other. Choose the mix of high-yield and growth-oriented stocks that is right for your desired income and how much risk you can handle. The advantage of this way is that your portfolio creates money as well as ensures your wealth grows steadily.

Make use of the tips and strategies to oversee and adjust your investments. Sign up for automatic notifications and use a plan that will make your dividends automatically renew your shares. Because of these systems, you can keep an eye on the important objectives and check that your investments are helping you reach them.

Taking part in the community is an important aspect of dividend investing. Get involved with communities of investors on the internet, help one another, and learn about the latest trends. Strong support networks can give you useful words of wisdom to guide you and encourage you when you've completed a challenging task.

Consider the significance of mixing different types of investments to minimize risks as you develop your portfolio. Allocate your funds among various areas and regions so that you can handle risks and benefit from opportunities in several markets. When you own various investments, not only are you protected, but your portfolio can also perform well in a variety of economies.

Be committed to the future that dividend investing calls for. Building financial independence takes time and, little by little, adds up to important achievements. Keep track of your developments frequently and praise yourself as you reach every financial target.

You should now be totally dedicated to practicing dividend investing. When your brokerage account is open and your stocks are chosen, you're ready to move ahead. Any dividend you get is another sign of your financial independence, thanks to being wise and consistent about your investments.

Keep to the ideas of dividend investment, and you will find yourself on the way to greater peace in your finances. You have the tools, you know the basics, and what you achieve moving forward depends on you. Take this day as the start of making your financial dreams come true.

Made in United States
North Haven, CT
29 December 2025

85952917R00055